The ABC's

(Antecedent-Behaviors-Consequences)

# of Response to Intervention & Behavior:

Next Steps

A Practitioner's Guide to Implementation

Outskirts Press, Inc.
Denver, Colorado

The A-B-C's of Response to Intervention & Behavior: Next Steps
A Practitioner's Guide to Implementation
All Rights Reserved.
Copyright © 2009 Cassandra Allen Holifield, PhD.
V4.0

Outskirts Press, Inc.
http://www.outskirtspress.com

ISBN: 978-1-4327-3649-1

Library of Congress Control Number: 2008939531

Outskirts Press and the "OP" logo are trademarks belonging to Outskirts Press, Inc.

PRINTED IN THE UNITED STATES OF AMERICA

About the Author

Dr. Cassandra Allen Holifield received her doctorate of philosophy (PhD.) in special education from Georgia State University in 2003 with a concentration in Emotional Behavioral Disorders, Specific Learning Disabilities and Autism. She now serves as the Director of Northwest Georgia Learning Resources System (GLRS), an extension of the Georgia Department of Education, directing and coordinating special education services for 16 local school systems in Northwest Georgia, the Northwest Georgia Network for Education and Therapeutic Support, and the Georgia School for the Deaf. Dr. Holifield previously served as the State Consultant for Emotional Behavioral Disorders for the Georgia Department of Education and also served as an active participant on the Continuous Improvement Monitoring Team.

Dr. Holifield also developed and coordinated two State Improvement Grants for the Georgia Department of Education, "The Emotional Behavior Disorder (EBD) Teacher Mentoring Academy, and "The School Wide Discipline/Effective Behavioral Intervention & Support (EBIS) Program". Additionally, Dr. Holifield served as a Special Education Ambassador to South Africa in 2005 and has been recognized by the Manchester National Who's Who Among Executives and Professionals in the field of Education in 2006.

Dr. Holifield is a nationally recognized presenter in the field of education, specializing in special education: "The Individuals with Disabilities Education Act (IDEA)", "No Child Left Behind (NCLB)", Collaboration/Inclusion, Differentiated Instruction, Positive Behavioral Supports, School-Wide Discipline, Emotional Behavioral Disorders, Specific Learning Disabilities, Autism, Disproportionality, Response to Intervention (RTI), and overall School Improvement.

Contact Information:
Cassandra Allen Holifield, PhD.
Email: Cassandra_allen@bellsouth.net or drcallen@allenconsultingpdfi.com
Website: www.allenconsultingdfi.com

Dedication

I dedicate the work of this book to children all over the world who are angry, misunderstood, unloved, neglected, forgotten, abandoned, abused, humiliated, hurt, taken for granted or almost completely destroyed by life and its circumstances. It is because of my unconditional love for you that I am able to love completely again. You saved my life and I want to save yours. Embrace your education and become the person you desire to be. Never let anyone tell you that "you can't" because "you can".

Acknowledgments

Special thanks to my best friend, soul mate, and loving husband, Len for his undying love, support and patience; to my son, Cameron for allowing me to "be" a mother, rather than just dreaming of being one; to my parents for always encouraging me to reach for the stars and to dream and think big; to my best friends for surrounding me with laughter and solace from a world sometimes filled with insanity; but most of all I give thanks to God, for loving me unconditionally, and for blessing me with exceedingly, abundantly above all that I can ask or think. It is because of God that I have hope, and this book was written, without HIM I am and have nothing.

Contents:

INTRODUCTION

First, I'd like to thank Dr. Robert J. Marzano for being a great researcher who had the foresight and genius to write what I consider to be one of his most important works, *"What Works in Schools: Translating Research into Action"* (Marzano, 2003). This book is a prototype of Marzano's work that represents a bound teacher friendly meta-analysis of educational research findings that created the new standard in education for utilizing research-based practices to guide instruction. Novel idea, absolutely not! But it was Dr. Marzano's body of work that challenged those in the ivory towers of education to do what we've already known to work and that is to finally construct and use "research to practice' as the standard in education.

As a result of the tremendous impact of Dr. Marzano's work had on my life as an educator, I have decided to follow his lead and write a practitioner's guide to Response to Intervention (RTI) and behavior based on research findings of "other" great researchers that is user friendly and practical for "real" educators, those still in the trenches, to use as a user friendly, practical, easy to follow, step-by-step guide to RTI implementation for students who exhibit challenging behaviors. The *"ABC's of RTI and Behavior"* is not intended to be a text book filled with excessive amounts of useless, meaningless research. The purpose of this book is to provide educators with a true resource for RTI and behavior implementation that makes sense and is based on research-findings that true researchers have conducted, that is effective for both teachers and students to achieve success in education. It is important that we recognize that in order for No Child to be Left Behind, we must Leave No Teacher Behind.

"Success is to be measured not so much by the position that one has reached in life as by the obstacles which he has overcome." Booker T. Washington

Chapter 1

RESPONSE TO INTERVENTION AND BEHAVIORISM

"Give me a dozen healthy infants, well-formed, and my own specified world to bring them up in and I'll guarantee to take any one at random and train him to become any type of specialist I might select - doctor, lawyer, artist, merchant-chief, and, yes, even beggar-man and thief, regardless of his talents, penchants, tendencies, abilities, vocations, and race of his ancestors." John B. Watson, Father of Behaviorism, 1930

The historical roots of "behaviorism" originated back in the early 20th century by a charismatic American psychologist by the name of John B. Watson. According to Watson, behavior can only be studied in a systematic and observable manner and it has no consideration of internal mental states. Behaviorism posits that all behavior, both adaptive and maladaptive, is acquired through learning and learning occurs as a result of the consequence of behavior. Behavior followed by pleasant consequences will be repeated and behavior followed by unpleasant behaviors will cease.

"The consequences of behavior determine the probability that the behavior will occur again." B. F. Skinner

Initially Watson, then B.F. Skinner strongly opposed the idea that psychological theories be based on "mental processes". Instead, they posited that psychology, emphasize the importance of empirical, observable behaviors. As a result, researchers began studying incidents that could be experienced empirically that could be agreed upon with reliability by multiple observers. Additionally, behavioral pioneers theorized that the principle determinant factor in behavior is determined by the external environment, and genetic predispositions are unimportant. So in the classic "nature vs. nurture" debate, behaviorists position themselves directly on the "nurture" side which remains important today with the evolution of Response to Intervention which clearly supports the side of nurture.

Response to Intervention (RTI) from a behaviorist perspective is nothing new. It's a common sense systematic approach to modifying behavior as used in "operant conditioning" in which behaviors can be changed by forming a relationship between a behavior and a consequence. Similarly, Response to Intervention can be an effective process for providing appropriate academic and behavioral instruction for "most" students, IF the student has a "won't do" problem as opposed to a "can't do" problem and there is direct relationship between a student's deficit area and the instructional intervention implemented to remediate the problem. Additionally, the intervention(s) must be implemented consistently with fidelity.

The purpose of *"The ABC's of RTI and Behavior"* is NOT to provide educational practitioners with a textbook of research on RTI. The purpose of this book is to provide practitioners with a step-by-step implementation guide to support students with challenging behaviors reach the goal of improved academic and behavioral achievement using both the standard treatment and problem solving approach to RTI.

In writing this book, I have decided to leave the research to the experts such as Dr. Joe Witt, Dr. Miyo Witt, Dr. Daniel Reschley, Dr. Doug Fuchs, Dr. Lynn Fuchs, Dr. George Sugai, Dr. Rob Horner, Dr. Jeffery Sprague, Jim Wright, Dr. Robert Marzano, Dr. John McCook, Cara Shores, Kim Chester, Dr. Laura Riffel, and countless others. However, I have decided to utilize a great deal of their research findings to write a user-friendly practitioners' guide for implementing RTI for students with challenging behaviors. It is my belief that educators will do what they need to do to help students learn if they know what to do. The purpose of this book is to show them how to do it.

Therefore, the layout of this book will begin with an overview of education law and essential terminology related to Response to Intervention. It is my intent for this to be the only "technical" writing presented in this book. All other chapters will proceed with a brief overview and explanation of the tiers represented in the three-tiered model of RTI along with practical implementation guidance on how to identify and provide appropriate behavioral and/or academic supports to students identified with a need.

Chapter 2
LAW, BEST PRACTICES, AND ESSENTIAL TERMINOLOGY

IDEA

The *"Individuals with Disabilities Education Act"* also known as Public Law 94-142 (PL 94-142), was passed in 1975 to improve educational opportunities for children with disabilities. The statute is typically reauthorized every five years and was most recently updated by President George W. Bush and passed on November 19, 2004 by Congress and is now known as the *"Individuals with Disabilities Education Improvement Act"* (*IDEIA* 2004; PL 108-446). The purpose for the passage of this ground-breaking legislation is to:

- Assure that all children with disabilities have available to them a "free appropriate public education" which puts an emphasis on special education and related services designed to meet the individual needs of students with disabilities

- Assure that the rights of children with disabilities and their parents are safeguarded

- Assist States and local school systems in making education available to all children with disabilities

- Accurately assess and ensure the efficacy of endeavors to educate all children with disabilities

The 1997 Amendments to *IDEA* expound upon its original purpose established in 1975 to include improving the results of children with disabilities and their families. *IDEA* 2004 maintains this focus and extended the focus by placing a greater emphasis on improving outcomes of children with disabilities and their families by highlighting the importance of stronger accountability for results. *(Individuals with Disabilities Education Improvement Act of 2004; Individuals with Disabilities Education Act of 1997; & Education for All Handicapped Children's Act of 1975)*

No Child Left Behind Act (NCLB)

President George W. Bush secured the passage of the momentous Public Law 107-110, also known as *"The No Child Left Behind Act"* in January of 2001, which reauthorized the *"Elementary and Secondary Education Act"* (ESEA) of 1965, Public Law 89-10. The *"No Child Left Behind Act"* is a bipartisan education reform Act that was formed out of President Bush's immense concern that too many of our nation's neediest children were being left behind despite $200 billion in Federal spending on educating these children since the passage of the

"Elementary and Secondary Education Act" of 1965. *"No Child Left Behind"* integrates the principles and strategies proposed by President Bush to include:

- *Increased Accountability for Results* in Title I schools requiring States to implement statewide accountability systems encompassing all public schools and students based on challenging State standards in core academic subjects for all students in grades 3-8 in which all groups of students should reach proficiency within 12 years. Assessments results and State progress objectives must be disaggregated by poverty, race/ethnicity, disability category, and limited English proficiency to ensure that no group is left behind

- *Increased Parental Choice for Parents and Students* attending Title I schools that fail to meet State standards. Parents of children in low-performing schools have new options under *"No Child Left Behind"*. In schools that do not meet state standards for at least two consecutive years, parents may transfer their children to a better-performing public school, including a public charter school, within their school district. The school district must provide transportation, using Title I funds if necessary. Students from low-income families in schools that fail to meet state standards for at least three years are eligible to receive supplemental educational services, including tutoring, after-school services, and summer school. Also students who attend a "persistently dangerous" school or are the victim of a violent crime while in their school have the option to attend a safe school within their district.

- *Increased Flexibility for States, School Districts and Schools* for unprecedented flexibility in the use of Federal education funds in exchange for stronger accountability of results. These new flexibility provisions allow States and local educational agencies to transfer up to 50 percent of the federal formula grant funds they receive under the Improving Teacher Quality State Grants, Educational Technology, Innovative Programs, and Safe and Drug-Free Schools programs to any one of these programs, or their Title I program, without separate approval. This allows districts to use funds for their particular needs, such as hiring new teachers, increasing teacher pay, and improving teacher training and professional development.

- *Proven Education Methods* through rigorous scientific research is a major emphasis of the *"No Child Left Behind Act"*. Federal funding is aimed at supporting these programs and teaching methods that succeed in improving student learning and achievement. President Bush under the *"No Child Left Behind Act"* has a personal commitment to ensure that every child can read by the end of the third grade. In an effort to accomplish this goal, the new *Reading First Initiative* significantly increases the Federal investment in supporting scientifically based reading instruction programs in the early grades. The *"No Child Left Behind Act"* fully implements President Bush's *Reading First Initiative* that will make six-year grants to States, which will make competitive sub-grants to local communities. Local recipients will administer screening and diagnostic assessments to determine which students grades K-3 are at risk of reading failure, and provide professional development for K-3 teachers in the essential components of reading instruction. One major benefit of implementing Reading First Initiatives in schools would be reduced identification of children for special education services due to a lack of appropriate reading instruction in their early years. (*The No Child Left Behind Act of 2001*; www.ed.gov).

DISPROPORTIONALITY

Since the enactment of the *Individuals with Disabilities Education Act (IDEA)* in 1975, approximately six million children with disabilities have been able to enjoy the rights to a "free appropriate public education" (FAPE). Unfortunately, the benefits of FAPE have not been equitably distributed among children from diverse backgrounds with outcomes resulting in the disproportionate representation of minority students in special education (Losen & Orfield, 2002). Disproportionality, also referred to, as Overrepresentation, has become an important and persistent topic in special education almost since its origin.

As a result of Disproportionality, an excessive number of minority children with disabilities have too often experienced inadequate services, poor instruction, lower-quality curriculum, and unnecessary seclusion from their non-disabled peers. These inappropriate practices have occurred in both general and special education classrooms and have resulted in overrepresentation, misclassification and educational disadvantages for many minority students, particularly Black children (Losen & Orfield, 2002; Project FORUM, 1997).

According to the 1997 data collected by the U.S. Department of Education Office of Civil Rights (1998), approximately 1.5 million minority children were identified as having mental retardation, emotional disturbance, or a specific learning disability. More than 876,000 of these children were Black or Native American. The research findings also indicated that Black or Native-American students were also significantly more likely than White students to be identified as having a disability. For example, in most states, African-American students were identified at one and a half times the rate of White children in the disability categories of mental retardation and emotional disturbance (Losen & Orfield, 2002)

Additionally, the National Research Council published a report that shows more than 14% of African-American students are in special education compared 13% American-Indian, 12% Whites, 11% Hispanics, and 5% Asian-Americans. The disparities are greatest in categories with the greatest stigma: 2.6% of Black students are identified as mentally retarded compared with 1.2% White students (Donovan & Cross, 2002).

It is imperative that researchers and educators take a closer look at why minority students are not performing academically and behaviorally to that of their same age peers before referring these students on for special education services. Many minority students experience academic difficulty and/or display behavioral problems in school. However, these problems do not necessarily stem from a disability. These problems could be related to factors such as a lack of educational exposure and opportunity, socioeconomic factors, inadequate educational experiences, different learning styles, cultural or linguistic differences and/or inappropriate curriculum and instructional practices (Garcia & Ortiz, 1988). These problems in and of themselves do not automatically necessitate special education services. It is extremely important that both administrators and educators understand that differences do not equate to deviance.

In an attempt to assess and remediate the overrepresentation of minority students in special education, the 1997 reauthorization of *IDEA* mandated new state reporting requirements concerning minority enrollment in special education and the supervision and expulsion of students with disabilities. The *IDEA* guarantees that students with disabilities are educated to the maximum extent appropriate in the least restrictive environment (LRE), which is presumed to be the general education classroom. This law was partly reauthorized to address race-based Disproportionality in special education programs. The section of *IDEA'97* applicable to this discussion reads:

300.755 Disproportionality

(a) General. Each state that receives assistance under Part B of the Act, and the Secretary of the Interior, shall provide for the collection and examination of data to determine if significant Disproportionality based on race is occurring in the State or in the schools operated by the Secretary of the Interior with respect to-
   (1) The identification of children as children with disabilities, including the identification of children as children with disabilities in accordance with a particular impairment described in section 602(3) of the Act; and
   (2) The placement in particular educational settings of these children.

(b) Review and revision of policies, practices, and procedures. In the case of a determination of significant Disproportionality with respect to the identification of children as children with disabilities, or the placement in particular educational settings of these children, in accordance with paragraph (a) of this section, the State or the Secretary of the Interior shall provide for the review and, if appropriate, revision of the policies, procedures, and practices used in the identification or placement to ensure that the policies, procedures, and practices comply with the requirements of Part B of the Act (Authority: 20 U.S. C. 1418(c)).

The *"Individuals with Disabilities Improvement Act"* of 2004 strengthens the previous statute's importance on the identification of Disproportionality. These changes include a more extensive examination of occurrences of Disproportionality, more widespread solutions where findings of Disproportionality occur, and a focus on the development of personnel preparation models to ensure appropriate placement and services for all students and to reduce Disproportionality in eligibility, placement, and disciplinary actions for minority and limited English proficient students.

Under *IDEA '97,* States examining Disproportionality are recommended to inspect their statewide data, but were not required to analyze data at the local educational agency level. Additionally, *IDEA 2004* specifies that where a determination of significant Disproportionality is found, the state education agency (SEA) shall provide for review and, if appropriate, revision of policies, procedures, and practices to ensure compliance with the requirements of *IDEA.* New provisions of the law additionally stipulate that LEAs may be required to reserve the maximum amount of funds under section 613(f) to provide comprehensive coordinated early intervening services, such as Response to Intervention (RTI), to serve students in the LEA, particularly students in groups that are significantly over-identified.

It is noteworthy to emphasize that Disproportionality has been shown to cause undue harm to minority students nationwide. Students are harmed due to being inappropriately labeled and placed in special education classrooms, which denies them access to the general education curriculum, resulting in their service needs not being appropriately addressed (*ILIAD Project, 2002*).

The question often arises, how is Disproportionality/Overrepresentation calculated? There are several formulas used to calculate Disproportionality; however, researchers do not agree on any one formula. One of the most common ways to calculate overrepresentation is to calculate the odds that students from one ethnic group have to be placed in a special education program compared to students from another ethnic group or compared to all other groups. For example, if you want to calculate the odds in which African-American students have been placed in Emotional Behavioral Disorder (EBD) classes compared to White students, follow these three steps: 1) Divide the number of African-American students placed in EBD classes by the total number of African-Americans at the school. This number tells you the percent of all African-American students at the school that are placed in EBD classes; 2) Divide the number of White students placed in EBD classes by the total number of White students at the school. This number indicates the percent of all White students at the school that are placed in EBD classes; and 3) Divide the score obtained in step 1 by the number obtained in step 2 to determine the odds African-American students have to be placed in EBD classes compared to White students. For example:

Step 1   50 (African-Americans students in EBD classes   = .20
          250 (All African-Americans students at the school)

Step 2   20 (White students in EBD classes)   = .05
          400 (All White students at the school)

Step 3   .20 (Percent of African-Americans student in EBD classes)   = 4.0
          .05 (Percent of White students in EBD classes)

When the number obtained in step 3 equals 1.0, it means both ethnic groups have equal chances to be placed in a special education program. If the number is greater than 1, it means African-Americans, in this example, would have greater odds than their White peers to be placed in EBD classes. In this example, the total score of 4 means that African-Americans are four times more likely than White students to be placed in EBD classes. Thus, you can conclude in this example that African-American students are over-represented in EBD classes at this school four times that of their White peers (Artiles & Harry, 2004).

PRE-REFERRAL INTERVENTIONS AND DISPROPORTIONALITY

Professional research suggests that student support teams, also referred to as pre-referral intervention teams, have the potential for preventing the over-identification and referral of minority students to special education. Pre-referral intervention teams when functioning effectively and efficiently have the potential to identify and address systematic problems that struggling and minority students face in school relating to academic and/or behavioral problems, inadequate instruction, irrelevant curriculum, cultural and/or linguistic related issues, lack of appropriate materials and resources and many other challenges that diverse students face.

Central to the purpose of student support teams and pre-referral intervention teams is to improve expectations and viewpoints of educational professionals to supplement and adequately address students' academic and behavioral needs. The pre-referral intervention process recognizes that numerous variables affect learning and research-based interventions are to be implemented that are specific to a student's deficit areas in order for improvement to occur. These interventions are to be implemented with the intent to assist students achieve academic and behavioral success within the general education classroom and are not put in place only as a stepping stone to refer a child on for special education services. It is essential that pre-referral team members DO NOT automatically assume that academic and behavioral difficulties lie within the child. They are to consider that an array of variables may be the source of the problem(s), including the curriculum, instructional delivery, instructional materials, instructional practices, teacher attitudes and expectations, perceptions, experiences, and cultural and linguistic issues that may affect a child's progress towards meeting the standards of the grade level general education curriculum.

The problem of race-based Disproportionality continues to be an escalating national concern for parents, students, and educators. In a response to reduce the disproportionate representation of culturally and linguistically diverse students being placed in special education due to inappropriate or ineffective practices, *The National Center for Culturally Responsive Educational Systems (NCCRESt)*, a project funded by the U.S. Department of Education's Office of Special Education Programs, was created to provide technical assistance and professional development to help close the achievement gap between students from culturally and linguistically diverse backgrounds and their peers to reduce inappropriate referrals to special education. The project targets improvements in culturally responsive practices, early intervention, literacy, and positive behavioral supports.

The basis of *NCCREST* is grounded in the assumption that disproportionate representation should be addressed through the creation of culturally responsive educational systems. The *National Center for Culturally Responsive Educational Systems* purpose is not to "fix" culturally and linguistically diverse students' deficits or professionals' biases, its purpose is to create conditions, produce resources, tools, and support multiple stakeholders in the creation of educational systems that are responsive to culturally responsive pedagogy (Artiles & Harry, 2004; Hilliard, 2000). Culturally responsive educational systems benefit ALL students, not just minority students and students with disabilities. The foundation of culturally responsive educational systems are grounded on the premise that culturally and linguistically diverse students can excel academically and behaviorally if their culture, language, heritage, and experiences are valued and are used to facilitate their learning and development. Additionally, these students perform on par with White students when they are provided equal access to highly qualified teachers, programs, research based curricula, resources and services in the least restrictive environment to the maximum extent appropriate, (www.nccrest.org, 2005).

EARLY INTERVENING SERVICES

The reauthorization of the *Individuals with Disabilities Education Improvement Act* (IDEA) was signed into law on December 3, 2004, by President George W. Bush. "Early Intervening Services" was added to the Statue under Local Educational Agency Eligibility in *IDEA* 2004. The provisions regarding "Early Intervening Services" of *IDEA* took effect on July 1, 2005 and refers to a broad application of support services and includes activities such as professional development, evaluation, and support for students who are not eligible for services under *IDEA* 2004.

"Early Intervening Services" are designed for students in kindergarten through twelfth grade, with a particular emphasis on students in kindergarten through grade 3, who have not been identified as needing special education or related services, but who need additional academic and behavioral support to succeed in the general education environment. The statute allows a local educational agency (LEA) to use not more than 15 percent of the amount it received under *IDEA* Part B for any fiscal year (less any amount reduced by the agency under Section 613(a)(2)(C)) in combination with other amounts, which may include amounts other than education funds, to develop and implement coordinated, early intervening services, which may include interagency financing structures.

Activities allowed in implementing coordinated, Early Intervening Services by local educational agencies (LEAs) include: 1) professional development, which may be provided by entities other than LEAs for teachers and other school staff to enable them to deliver scientifically-based literacy instruction and, when appropriate, instruction on the use of adaptive and instructional software; and 2) providing educational and behavioral evaluations, services and supports, including scientifically-based literacy instruction.

In the case of the identification of significant Disproportionality with respect to the identification of children as children with disabilities, or the placement in particular educational settings of such children, in accordance with Section 618(d)(1), the state or the Secretary of the Interior will require an LEA identified under Section 618(d)(1) to reserve the maximum amount of funds under Section 613(f) to provide comprehensive coordinated early intervening services to children in such LEA, particularly children in those groups that were significantly over-identified…[618(d)(2)(B)]. (www.ed.gov/about/offices/list/osers/index.html, 2005)

RESPONSE TO INTERVENTION (RTI)

The reauthorization of the *Individuals with Disabilities Education Improvement Act* of 2004 allows for the use of Response to Intervention (RTI) as an alternative to discrepancy-based models for the identification of specific learning disabilities (SLD). The IQ-achievement discrepancy approach used in identifying students with or without Specific Learning Disabilities (SLD) has been criticized for decades for its use in making eligibility determinations. Many researchers who are opposed to the IQ-achievement discrepancy model document that discrepant and non-discrepant low achievers are not meaningfully different in areas of achievement, behavior, or processes related to reading. Additionally, discrepant and non-discrepant low achievers do not differ in their response to instruction nor does the discrepancy approach provide specific instructional information that can be used to improve instruction (Gresham, VanDerHeyden, & Witt, 2005).

Response to Intervention as described by Fiona James proposes changes in how children with SLD are identified moving from the old model of "Wait to Fail" to the new preventive RTI model, which monitors student progress early with different levels of intervention intensity using data generated from those interventions to make instructional and eligibility decisions.

Even though some states have adopted four or more tiers of intervention for their RTI model, the most well-known and referenced model is often referred to as the "Three-Tiered Model" of RTI. The three-tier model of RTI will be the primary referenced used in this manual. Tier 1 involves assessing all students using periodic (e.g. Fall, Winter, Spring) curriculum based measures (CBM) to establish benchmarks for early identification within the general education classroom to determine if a child is on grade level. Tier II involves strategically monitoring at-risk students' academic and/or behavioral progress on a more frequent basis (e.g. monthly, bi-monthly) while also monitoring the fidelity of implementation, the effectiveness of instructional changes being implemented using research based pre-referral interventions that focus on remediation of students' specific needs. Tier III, in the national model, involves conducting a comprehensive evaluation and developing intensive instructional interventions using individualized intervention for children who are intervention resistant while monitoring progress to determine if special education services are needed. Other states such as Georgia have implemented a four-tier model of RTI and Tier III is representative of Student Support Team interventions for intervention resistant students taking place in the general education setting, and Tier IV is reserved for students who have been identified as needing Special Education or Gifted services.

Public Health & Disease Prevention
Kutash et al., 2006; Larson, 1994

- ## Tertiary (FEW)
  - Reduce complications, intensity, severity of current cases

- ## Secondary (SOME)
  - Reduce current cases of problem behavior

- ## Primary (ALL)
  - Reduce new cases of problem behavior

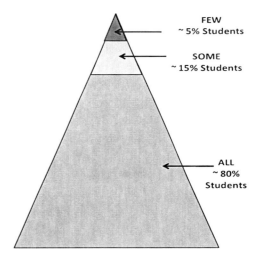

Continuum of Effective Behavior Support

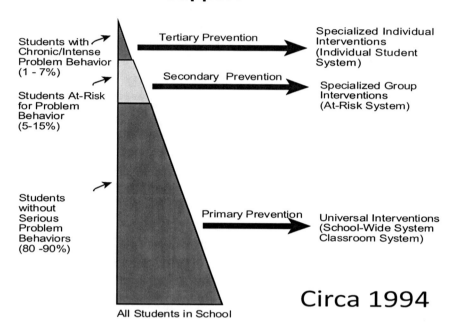

Students with Chronic/Intense Problem Behavior (1 - 7%)

Students At-Risk for Problem Behavior (5-15%)

Students without Serious Problem Behaviors (80 -90%)

Tertiary Prevention → Specialized Individual Interventions (Individual Student System)

Secondary Prevention → Specialized Group Interventions (At-Risk System)

Primary Prevention → Universal Interventions (School-Wide System Classroom System)

Circa 1994

All Students in School

Designing School-Wide Systems for Student Success

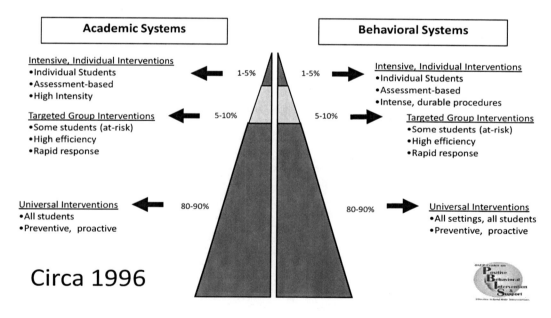

Academic Systems

Intensive, Individual Interventions
•Individual Students
•Assessment-based
•High Intensity

1-5%

Targeted Group Interventions
•Some students (at-risk)
•High efficiency
•Rapid response

5-10%

Universal Interventions
•All students
•Preventive, proactive

80-90%

Behavioral Systems

1-5%

Intensive, Individual Interventions
•Individual Students
•Assessment-based
•Intense, durable procedures

5-10%

Targeted Group Interventions
•Some students (at-risk)
•High efficiency
•Rapid response

80-90%

Universal Interventions
•All settings, all students
•Preventive, proactive

Circa 1996

(Sugai, Horner, Gresham, 2002)

RTI Terminology

Curriculum Based Measurement (CBM)

Curriculum Based Measurement (CBM) is a highly researched method of monitoring student progress that directly assesses basic academic skills typically in the areas of student readiness, reading, spelling, written expression, and mathematics. Curriculum based measures are generally administered by a classroom teacher using standardized instructions in which brief, timed, assessments are given that have been taken from the local school system's curriculum to monitor student progress.

Data Based Decision Making

Data-based decision making is critical to the RTI problem solving process. It involves reviewing student response and intervention fidelity in order to make the decision to continue, increase, decrease, or change academic or behavioral supports.

Evidenced Based or Scientifically Validated Interventions

The No Child Left Behind Act defines scientifically-based research as "research that involves the application of rigorous, systematic, and objective procedures to obtain reliable and valid knowledge relevant to education activities and programs".

Progress Monitoring

Progress monitoring is a scientifically-based practice that is used to assess students' academic and/or behavioral performance. Results are used to evaluate the effectiveness of interventions on student progress towards identified areas of weakness. Progress monitoring can be implemented on individual students, an entire classroom, or an entire grade level of students.

Problem Solving Treatment Model

The problem solving treatment model is a classroom based intervention approach to RTI that involves customized decision making based on a student's individual needs. Intervention teams at the school or district level make decisions about the need for interventions, the specific interventions to be used, progress monitoring schedule, and evaluating the effectiveness of the intervention (Wright, 2007; Bender & Shores, 2007, McCook, 2006).

Standard Treatment Protocol Model

The standard treatment protocol model is a highly standardized, stand-alone, research validated intervention approach (standard protocol) used for groups of students identified as having the same learning problem. Services for these students, generally takes place outside of the general education classroom (Wright, 2007; Bender & Shores, 2007).

Treatment Fidelity

Fidelity of implementation is the delivery of instruction in the way it was designed to be delivered (Gresham, MacMillan, Boebe-Frankenberger, & Bocian, 2000). It is essential that fidelity address the integrity with which screening and progress-monitoring procedures are completed and an explicit decision-making model is followed. In an RTI model, fidelity is important at both the school level (e.g., implementation of the process) and the teacher level (e.g., implementation of instruction and progress monitoring) (www.nrcld.org, August 2006).

There are numerous other essential terms related to RTI that will be introduced through this book. These terms are introduced now to provide you with a frame of reference and a foundation for understanding RTI.

Chapter 3

EXCLUSIONARY FACTORS

In determining special education eligibility, the intervention team must ensure that the identified area of concern is not the primary concern of:

- Cultural factors
- Environmental or economic disadvantage
- Limited English proficiency
- Visual, hearing, or motor disability
- Lack of appropriate instruction in reading, including the essential components of reading instruction
- Lack of appropriate instruction in math

A child must NOT be determined to be a child with a disability, if the determinant factor is a result of one or more of the above-referenced areas or if the child does not otherwise meet the area of eligibility criteria for a child with a disability. Other essential questions that must be considered and documented prior to determining special education eligibility include:

- Were appropriate research-based interventions provided for a sufficient amount of time for the student to make progress in the general education curriculum?
- Is the child's primary language English?
- Does the student have irregular attendance problems that negatively impact the student's ability to make adequate progress towards the grade level curriculum?
- Is there a summary of interventions tried related to the student's deficit area provided prior to being referred for special education services?
- Is there a summary of progress monitoring data provided documenting the student's academic and/or behavioral achievement towards the standards?
- Is the child's academic and/or behavioral data atypical from that compared to peers of similar socioeconomic status and ethnicity? (Georgia Department of Education, 2007).

Exclusionary Factors

General for all areas: 160-4-7-.05(2)(c)

A child must not be determined to be a child with a disability if the primary factor for that determination is –

1. Lack of appropriate instruction in reading, including the essential components of reading instruction as defined in section 1208(3) of ESEA);
2. Lack of appropriate instruction in mathematics; or
3. Limited English proficiency; and
4. If the child does not otherwise meet the eligibility criteria under this Rule [34 C.F.R. §300.306(b)(1)-(2)]

ELIGIBILITY CATEGORY	REQUIRED DATA
Emotional & Behavioral Disorder	• Documentation of comprehensive prior extension of services available in the regular program to include counseling, modifications of the regular program or alternative placement available to all children, and data-based progress monitoring of the results of interventions. • Exclusion factors – --Lack of appropriate instruction in reading including the essential components of reading instruction; --Lack of instruction in math; --Lack of instruction in writing --Limited English proficiency --Visual, hearing, or motor disability --Intellectual disabilities --Cultural factors --Environmental factors or economic disadvantage --Atypical educational history (multiple school attendance, lack of attendance, etc.
Intellectual Disability	• Exclusion factors— --Lack of appropriate instruction in reading, including the essential components of reading instruction; --Lack of appropriate instruction in math;

	--Lack of appropriate instruction in written expression -- Limited English proficiency --Visual, hearing, or motor disability --Intellectual disabilities --Cultural factors --Environmental factors or economic disadvantage --Atypical educational history (multiple school attendance, lack of attendance, etc.
Other Health Impaired	▪ Exclusion factors— --Lack of appropriate instruction in reading, including the essential components of reading instruction; --Lack of appropriate instruction in math; --Lack of appropriate instruction in writing --Limited English proficiency --Visual, hearing, or motor disability --Intellectual disabilities --Cultural factors --Environmental factors or economic disadvantage --Atypical educational history (multiple school attendance, lack of attendance, etc.
Significant Development Delay	▪ For children who are kindergarten age or older, initial eligibility shall include documented evidence of that impact on education performance is not due to: ▪ Exclusion factors— --Lack of appropriate instruction in reading or literacy readiness, including the essential components of reading instruction -Lack of appropriate instruction in math or math readiness skills - Limited English proficiency - Visual, hearing, or motor disability -Emotional disturbances -Cultural factors or -Environmental or economic disadvantage
Specific Learning Disability	▪ Exclusion factors— --Lack of appropriate instruction in reading, to include the essential components of reading instruction (phonemic instruction, phonics, fluency, vocabulary, and comprehension

	- Lack of appropriate instruction in math -Lack of appropriate instruction in writing -Limited English proficiency -Visual, hearing, or motor disability -Intellectual disabilities -Emotional disturbances -Cultural factors -Environmental or economic disadvantage or -Atypical educational history (such as irregular school attendance, or attendance at multiple schools)
Speech Language Impairment	▪ Exclusion factors— --Environmental, cultural, or economic disadvantage cannot be ruled out as primary factors causing the impairment or --A child exhibits inconsistent, situational, transitory, or developmental speech language difficulties that children experience at various times and to various degrees --Because children who have communication difficulties do not necessarily have speech or language impairments, the speech language impairment program may not be the appropriate service delivery model to adequately meet the child's education needs. For this reason, all children suspected of having communication problems shall be the subject of a Student Support Team (SST) to problem solve and implement strategies to determine and limit the adverse effect on the child's education performance.

Chapter 4

UNIVERSAL SCREENING

Response to intervention (RTI), patterned after public-health models is a process frequently used to prevent chronic learning and/or behavior problems. Essential first steps in the RTI prevention model is the process of universal screening (screening of all students) to identify students who are at risk for learning and/or behavioral problems. Therefore, accuracy in identification of which students warrant further assistance is key.

Universal screening is also essential in determining whether or not a student is "at risk". In order to determine which students are "at-risk", a cut score on a screening measure must be predetermined. A cut score is simply a score that divides students "not at risk" with those who may be "potentially at risk". For example, students who score below a norm-referenced cut point (e.g. less than the 25th percentile on the Woodcock Reading Mastery Tests – Word Identification), or below a performance benchmark associated with poor long-term results (e.g. less than 15 on a curriculum-based measurement of reading fluency at the beginning of first grade), or students who miss 3 or more days within the first 9 weeks of school and are at risk of failing a class, may enter into a Tier 2 intervention.

Regarding best practice for school-wide screening within an RTI model, Fuchs & Fuchs (2006) recommend that schools use school-wide screening in combination with at least five weeks of weekly progress monitoring within the general education classroom to identify students who require preventive intervention because one-time universal screening at the beginning of the year can over-identify students who require preventive intervention. To support these findings, Compton et al., (2006) show that five weeks of weekly progress monitoring can reduce or even eliminate the provision of preventative intervention of these "false positives".

Universal screenings also play a critical role in determining "what" constitutes being "at risk" which is generally determined by using a criterion referenced or a normative referenced standard of performance for academics and number of absences, office referrals, or suspensions in conjunction with poor academic performance help to determine what constitutes being behaviorally "at-risk".

A criterion standard of performance refers to a specific level of mastery or proficiency on a specific skill. A normative referenced standard of performance refers to screening results that are compared to that of other age/grade level students with comparisons being made. Criterion measures are preferred because they provide more accurate information about performance on relevant skills (National Research Center on Learning Disabilities [NRCLD], 2006). Both criterion standards of performance and normative standards of performance can be used to establish behavioral expectations for screening.

In general, universal screenings consist of a quick assessment of grade level academic and/or behavioral critical skills (e.g. phonemic awareness, reading fluency, math computation, tardiness, absenteeism, suspension, non-compliance, etc.). Teachers use these screening measures to identify students who meet the criteria for possibly being "at risk". Students identified as being "at risk" are then considered for more intensive assessment. However, in order for a screening measure to be useful, it should meet three criteria (Jenkins, 2003):

1. It should identify students who require further assessment.
2. It should be practical.
3. It should accurately identify students in a timely manner without using resources that could be used more effectively elsewhere.

Universal screenings are not to be used as a one-time process that takes place once during the school year. Screenings are to be conducted several times over the course of the school year and across grade levels throughout the school year. Best practices indicate that school-wide universal screenings are to take place at least three times per year during the fall, winter, and spring to identify students' levels of academic and/or behavioral proficiency. Once universal screening data is available, it is to be organized so comparison of both group and individual performance on specific skills can be made (National Association of State Directors of Special Education [NASDSE], 2005). When universal screening data is disaggregated and analyzed in this manner, universal screening data serves three main purposes:

1. To identify individual students in need of Tier 2 interventions
2. To provide intervention teams on class-wide performance so building administrators can provide assistance to specific teachers who may need additional support
3. To provide additional opportunities to identify students who may slip through the cracks when only one screening is conducted
Following is a table of step-by-step instructions for implementing RTI &

Behavior in Tier 1. This table is to be used as a guide for implementation along with the sample data collection forms.

Steps in the RTI & Behavior Implementation Process
Tier 1

Tier 1	Tier 1 is the provision of effective evidenced-based instructional practices including school-wide behavior supports that involve All students, ALL staff, ALL settings, ALL year.
Focus of Tier 1	The focus of Tier 1 is on fidelity to the provision of high-quality evidenced-based instruction and school-wide behavioral supports using a validated core curriculum aligned with state standards and grade level expectations and interventions matched to student need.
Examples of data to be examined	Discipline/office referrals, attendance, tardies, suspensions, grades, test scores (formal & informal), juvenile justice records, family crisis (homelessness, divorce, death, unemployment, abuse, neglect, etc. – use professional judgment)
What happens at Tier 1	<ul><li>Primary prevention – used to keep problems from emerging</li><li>Applied to everyone in the same manner to the same degree</li><li>Interventions planned and implemented by general education teachers</li><li>Interventions benefit both high and low risk students</li><li>Behavioral expectations are defined</li><li>Behavioral expectations are taught</li><li>Reward system for appropriate behavior is provided</li><li>Continuum of consequences for problem behavior is provided</li><li>Continuous collection and use of data for decision-making by data analysis teams (e.g. grade level teams or content area teams)</li><li>Core instructional program taught using scientifically validated curriculum that is provided to ALL students</li><li>Differentiated instruction with the core instructional program that meets the needs of a wide range of students' needs</li><li>Interventions provided should bring large numbers of students to acceptable levels of proficiency</li><li>Students are progress monitored frequently (e.g. every 6 weeks with weekly progress monitoring using specific assessments related to the student's identified areas of concern)</li><li>Instructional and behavioral changes are based on student response</li><li>Duties and responsibilities are assigned</li><li>Types of data to be brought to the next meeting is determined</li><li>Dates for next meeting are determined</li><li>Students who continue to fall behind are identified for Tier 2 supports</li></ul>

Examples of Tier 1 Interventions	• Proactive school-wide positive behavior supports • Teach and encourage positive school-wide expectations • Effective classroom behavior management plans • Token economy • Group contingency management • Conflict resolution training • Violence prevention training • Validated core academic curriculum • Differentiation • Establish rules and consequences • Verbal and/or visual cueing • Parent engagement • Effective instruction
Steps to Implementing Tier 1	
Step 1	Conduct Behavioral Universal Screenings on ALL Students (Fall, Winter, & Spring)
Step 2	Document results and use assessment data to make instructional and behavioral decisions. It is important to document students' expected levels of performance and actual levels of performance and what students know and what they don't know, in order to provide high quality instruction. Examples of data sources: attendance records, discipline records (e.g. number of suspensions, expulsions, office referrals, non-compliance, etc.), semester grades, results of curriculum based measurements (CBM), progress monitoring, formative, summative and/or diagnostic assessments, etc.

Step 3	Disaggregate and analyze data:
	• 1st at the school-wide level
	• 2nd at the class-wide/grade-level
	• 3rd at the teacher level
	• 4th at the individual student level
	  1. Chart whole group data
	  2. Include date, teacher's name, school/district, grade level, content area or behavioral measure screened, performance level, expected level, end of the year benchmark performance level, etc.

Step 4	Identify students needing targeted group interventions/Tier 2 (e.g. those performing at or below the lowest 20%; or students performing at or below the 25th percentile on a screening measure; or students performing at or below a pre-determined cut score) from those meeting benchmark/Tier 1, etc.
	• General Rule of Thumb Part 1 – If more than 20% of the students in the general education classroom ARE NOT making acceptable progress in relation to the desired state benchmarks, then the school/district needs to improve the overall curriculum and/or instructional program (academic and/or behavioral) and no students should be referred on for Tier 2 interventions. This is a red flag that there is a bigger problem than an individual student problem. Intervention teams should look further at the effectiveness of the school-wide discipline plan, general classroom management plan, skill set of the teacher, etc.)
	• General Rule of Thumb Part 2 - If less than 20% of the students in the general education classroom ARE NOT making satisfactory progress, it can be presumed that the foundational program is sufficiently effective and further individualized interventions are needed at Tier 2 for students who are not meeting expectations of level of skills and progress
Step 5	Know, document, and be able to justify criteria and rationale for selection of students identified as needing Tier 2 interventions based on data. For example, all students scoring below the 25th percentile or designated cut score on a universal academic and/or behavioral screening are identified for Tier 2 supports.
Step 6	• Identify students in need of Tier 2 interventions • Complete the Universal Screening & Tier 1 Primary Prevention Data Collection Forms • Complete the Comprehensive At-Risk Questionnaire ONLY on students referred to Tier 2 • Review and complete as needed all other relevant universal screening and Tier 1 recommended forms • Complete any other district or state level required documents for Tier 1

Behavioral Universal Screening
Data Collection Table

Teachers' Name: _____

Grade Level: _____

Name of School & System: _____

Circle Type of Class: General   Co-Taught/Inclusion   Special   Other: _____

Directions: List the names of the students in your class. Document the number of absences, office referrals, out-of-school suspensions, in-school suspension, and failing courses for every student. Universal screening data is to be collected at least 3 times per year (Fall, Winter, Spring). Red Flag may require intervention.

Red Flag: 1) Fall – 3 or more total in any category; 2) Winter – 5 or more total in any category; 3) Winter – 7 or more total in any category

Key: # of Absences (AB)   # of Office Referrals (OR)   # of Out of School Suspensions (OSS)

    # of In-School Suspensions (ISS)   # of Failing Classes (FC)

Student's Name	Fall	Winter	Spring
	# AB = _____ # OR = _____ #OSS = _____ # ISS = _____ # FC = _____ Beginning of the Year/1st 9 weeks of school – Months (Aug. – Oct.) Date: _____	# AB = _____ # OR = _____ #OSS = _____ # ISS = _____ # FC = _____ Middle of the Year/2nd 9 weeks of school – Months (Nov. – Jan.) Date: _____	# AB = _____ # OR = _____ #OSS = _____ # ISS = _____ # FC = _____ End of the Year/3rd 9 weeks of school – Months (Feb. – April) Date: _____
1.	# AB = _____ # OR = _____ #OSS = _____ # ISS = _____ # FC = _____	# AB = _____ # OR = _____ #OSS = _____ # ISS = _____ # FC = _____	# AB = _____ # OR = _____ #OSS = _____ # ISS = _____ # FC = _____
2.	# AB = _____ # OR = _____ #OSS = _____ # ISS = _____ # FC = _____	# AB = _____ # OR = _____ #OSS = _____ # ISS = _____ # FC = _____	# AB = _____ # OR = _____ #OSS = _____ # ISS = _____ # FC = _____
3	# AB = _____ # OR = _____ #OSS = _____ # ISS = _____ # FC = _____	# AB = _____ # OR = _____ #OSS = _____ # ISS = _____ # FC = _____	# AB = _____ # OR = _____ #OSS = _____ # ISS = _____ # FC = _____

4.	# AB = _____ # OR = _____ #OSS = _____ # ISS = _____ # FC = _____	# AB = _____ # OR = _____ #OSS = _____ # ISS = _____ # FC = _____	# AB = _____ # OR = _____ #OSS = _____ # ISS = _____ # FC = _____
5.	# AB = _____ # OR = _____ #OSS = _____ # ISS = _____ # FC = _____	# AB = _____ # OR = _____ #OSS = _____ # ISS = _____ # FC = _____	# AB = _____ # OR = _____ #OSS = _____ # ISS = _____ # FC = _____
6.	# AB = _____ # OR = _____ #OSS = _____ # ISS = _____ # FC = _____	# AB = _____ # OR = _____ #OSS = _____ # ISS = _____ # FC = _____	# AB = _____ # OR = _____ #OSS = _____ # ISS = _____ # FC = _____
7.	# AB = _____ # OR = _____ #OSS = _____ # ISS = _____ # FC = _____	# AB = _____ # OR = _____ #OSS = _____ # ISS = _____ # FC = _____	# AB = _____ # OR = _____ #OSS = _____ # ISS = _____ # FC = _____
8.	# AB = _____ # OR = _____ #OSS = _____ # ISS = _____ # FC = _____	# AB = _____ # OR = _____ #OSS = _____ # ISS = _____ # FC = _____	# AB = _____ # OR = _____ #OSS = _____ # ISS = _____ # FC = _____
9.	# AB = _____ # OR = _____ #OSS = _____ # ISS = _____ # FC = _____	# AB = _____ # OR = _____ #OSS = _____ # ISS = _____ # FC = _____	# AB = _____ # OR = _____ #OSS = _____ # ISS = _____ # FC = _____
10.	# AB = _____ # OR = _____ #OSS = _____ # ISS = _____ # FC = _____	# AB = _____ # OR = _____ #OSS = _____ # ISS = _____ # FC = _____	# AB = _____ # OR = _____ #OSS = _____ # ISS = _____ # FC = _____
11.	# AB = _____ # OR = _____ #OSS = _____ # ISS = _____ # FC = _____	# AB = _____ # OR = _____ #OSS = _____ # ISS = _____ # FC = _____	# AB = _____ # OR = _____ #OSS = _____ # ISS = _____ # FC = _____
12.	# AB = _____ # OR = _____ #OSS = _____ # ISS = _____ # FC = _____	# AB = _____ # OR = _____ #OSS = _____ # ISS = _____ # FC = _____	# AB = _____ # OR = _____ #OSS = _____ # ISS = _____ # FC = _____

13.	# AB = _____ # OR = _____ #OSS = _____ # ISS = _____ # FC = _____	# AB = _____ # OR = _____ #OSS = _____ # ISS = _____ # FC = _____	# AB = _____ # OR = _____ #OSS = _____ # ISS = _____ # FC = _____
14.	# AB = _____ # OR = _____ #OSS = _____ # ISS = _____ # FC = _____	# AB = _____ # OR = _____ #OSS = _____ # ISS = _____ # FC = _____	# AB = _____ # OR = _____ #OSS = _____ # ISS = _____ # FC = _____
15.	# AB = _____ # OR = _____ #OSS = _____ # ISS = _____ # FC = _____	# AB = _____ # OR = _____ #OSS = _____ # ISS = _____ # FC = _____	# AB = _____ # OR = _____ #OSS = _____ # ISS = _____ # FC = _____
16.	# AB = _____ # OR = _____ #OSS = _____ # ISS = _____ # FC = _____	# AB = _____ # OR = _____ #OSS = _____ # ISS = _____ # FC = _____	# AB = _____ # OR = _____ #OSS = _____ # ISS = _____ # FC = _____
17.	# AB = _____ # OR = _____ #OSS = _____ # ISS = _____ # FC = _____	# AB = _____ # OR = _____ #OSS = _____ # ISS = _____ # FC = _____	# AB = _____ # OR = _____ #OSS = _____ # ISS = _____ # FC = _____
18.	# AB = _____ # OR = _____ #OSS = _____ # ISS = _____ # FC = _____	# AB = _____ # OR = _____ #OSS = _____ # ISS = _____ # FC = _____	# AB = _____ # OR = _____ #OSS = _____ # ISS = _____ # FC = _____
19.	# AB = _____ # OR = _____ #OSS = _____ # ISS = _____ # FC = _____	# AB = _____ # OR = _____ #OSS = _____ # ISS = _____ # FC = _____	# AB = _____ # OR = _____ #OSS = _____ # ISS = _____ # FC = _____
20.	# AB = _____ # OR = _____ #OSS = _____ # ISS = _____ # FC = _____	# AB = _____ # OR = _____ #OSS = _____ # ISS = _____ # FC = _____	# AB = _____ # OR = _____ #OSS = _____ # ISS = _____ # FC = _____
21.	# AB = _____ # OR = _____ #OSS = _____ # ISS = _____ # FC = _____	# AB = _____ # OR = _____ #OSS = _____ # ISS = _____ # FC = _____	# AB = _____ # OR = _____ #OSS = _____ # ISS = _____ # FC = _____

22.	# AB = _____ # OR = _____ #OSS = _____ # ISS = _____ # FC = _____	# AB = _____ # OR = _____ #OSS = _____ # ISS = _____ # FC = _____	# AB = _____ # OR = _____ #OSS = _____ # ISS = _____ # FC = _____
23.	# AB = _____ # OR = _____ #OSS = _____ # ISS = _____ # FC = _____	# AB = _____ # OR = _____ #OSS = _____ # ISS = _____ # FC = _____	# AB = _____ # OR = _____ #OSS = _____ # ISS = _____ # FC = _____
24.	# AB = _____ # OR = _____ #OSS = _____ # ISS = _____ # FC = _____	# AB = _____ # OR = _____ #OSS = _____ # ISS = _____ # FC = _____	# AB = _____ # OR = _____ #OSS = _____ # ISS = _____ # FC = _____
25.	# AB = _____ # OR = _____ #OSS = _____ # ISS = _____ # FC = _____	# AB = _____ # OR = _____ #OSS = _____ # ISS = _____ # FC = _____	# AB = _____ # OR = _____ #OSS = _____ # ISS = _____ # FC = _____

ABC's of RTI & Behavior
Research-Based Tiered Intervention Resource List

School: _____

District: _____

Date: _____

List at least 3 research-based interventions for Tiers 1, 2, & 3 in the areas of Reading, Math, Behavior, & Communication.

	Reading	Math	Behavior	Communication
Universal Screening Instruments:	1. 2. 3.	1. 2. 3.	1. 2. 3.	1. 2. 3.
Tier 1:	1. 2. 3.	1. 2. 3.	1. 2. 3.	1. 2. 3.
Tier 2:	1. 2. 3.	1. 2. 3.	1. 2. 3.	1. 2. 3.
Tier 3:	1. 2. 3.	1. 2. 3.	1. 2. 3.	1. 2. 3.

Local School System Response to Intervention Criteria for Selection
Tiers of Intervention

Name the universal screening instrument and tiered intervention used in each area. Then describe the criteria for identifying students in need of Tier 2 & 3 interventions in the areas of Reading, Math, Behavior, and/or Communication. Describe how these students were selected and the criteria for entering and exiting each Tier.

	Reading:	Math:	Behavior:	Communication:
Universal Screening Instrument(s):				
Tier 1 (All):	Expected Performance Level for Tier 1:	Expected Performance Level for Tier 1:	Expected Performance Level for Tier 1:	Expected Performance Level for Tier 1:
Tier 2 (Targeted):	Criteria for Entering Tier 2: Criteria for Exiting Tier 2 and Back to Tier1: Criteria for Remaining in Tier 2:	Criteria for Entering Tier 2: Criteria for Exiting Tier 2 and Back to Tier1: Criteria for Remaining in Tier 2:	Criteria for Entering Tier 2: Criteria for Exiting Tier 2 and Back to Tier1: Criteria for Remaining in Tier 2:	Criteria for Entering Tier 2: Criteria for Exiting Tier 2 and Back to Tier1: Criteria for Remaining in Tier 2:
Tier 3 (Individualized):	Criteria for Entering Tier 3: Criteria for Exiting Tier 3 and Back to Tier 2: Criteria for Remaining in Tier 3:	Criteria for Entering Tier 3: Criteria for Exiting Tier 3 and Back to Tier 2: Criteria for Remaining in Tier 3:	Criteria for Entering Tier 3: Criteria for Exiting Tier 3 and Back to Tier 2: Criteria for Remaining in Tier 3:	Criteria for Entering Tier 3: Criteria for Exiting Tier 3 and Back to Tier 2: Criteria for Remaining in Tier 3:

ABC's of Response to Intervention (RTI)
Data Collection & Intervention Documentation Forms

Student's Name: _____ Grade: _____
Date of Birth: _____ Student ID#: _____
School & District: _____ Homeroom Teacher: _____ Content: _____

	Universal Screening Process (All Students are Screened)
Who:	Ex. Homeroom, General, Special Education, or Content Area Teacher (Include grade level and/or content area taught) Specify:
What:	Ex. Core Content Areas (Reading, Math, Behavior, Communication, etc.) Ex. Screening Measure (Curriculum Based Measure (CBM) and/or or Behavioral Measure (Office referrals, attendance, suspensions, fights, expulsions, discipline records, previous year's test scores, grades, etc.) Specify:
Where:	Ex. Homeroom, General, Special Education, Early Intervention, Inclusion Class, or other Specify:
How:	Ex. School-wide or Class-wide Assessment Specify:
Time:	Ex. Quick Assessments (1 minute reading fluency probe, 2 minute 5th grade math fluency probe, number of office referrals within the 1st month of school, etc.) Specify:
Assessment:	Ex. 3 Times Per Year (Fall, Winter, & Spring) Specify with date:
Names of Identified Struggling Students & Description of the Problem:	
Struggling Students' Current Performance Level & Criteria Used to Identify Struggling Students (ex. students scoring in the bottom 25th percentile):	
Universal Screening Instruction/ Intervention Goal:	

Instruction/ Intervention Options:	• Option 1: • Option 2: • Option 3:

Universal Screening Instruction/ Intervention Dates (Fall, Winter, Spring) and Content Area(s) Screened:	• Type of universal screening(s) implemented & brief description:
	
	 • Exact Screening Date(s) & Content Area(s) Screened:
	   1. Content Area Screened & Date: _____
	   2. Content Area Screened & Date: _____
	   3. Content Area Screened & Date: _____

Person(s) Responsible for Implementing Instruction/ Intervention, Title, Name of Intervention, Length of Intervention, Location of Services, and Follow-Up Date(s):	• Name: • Title: • Location: • Name of Intervention: • Length of Intervention: • Location of Service: • Follow-Up Date(s):
Fidelity & Validity Statement:	• I certify that the above-referenced Universal Screening intervention/instruction was implemented consistently and reliably as described. _____ Signature, Title, & Date of Person(s) Responsible for Implementing the Universal Screening Instruction/Intervention
Universal Screening Results of Identified Struggling Students & Evaluation Criteria: (see progress monitoring graphs)	• Performance Level: • Rate of Growth: • Evaluation Criteria:
Team Decision & Explanation of Students Identified as Struggling by the Universal Screening:	❑ Tier 1 instruction/intervention successful ❑ Problem has not been resolved but progress is being made – continue with Tier 1 instruction/intervention using differentiation ❑ Problem not resolved MODIFY Tier 1 instruction/intervention/strategies ❑ Problem not resolved CHANGE Tier 1 instruction/intervention/strategies to: _____ ❑ Problem not resolved performance level and/or rate of growth remain below

	acceptable levels – initiate Tier 2 instruction/intervention ❑ Brief Explanation of Team Decision:

ABC' of Response to Intervention (RTI)
Data Collection & Intervention Documentation Forms

Student's Name: _____ Grade: _____
Date of Birth: _____ Student ID#: _____
School & District: _____ Homeroom Teacher: _____ Content: _____

	Tier 1 – Primary Prevention (Preventative & Proactive Interventions: Use this form to document preliminary research based interventions ONLY on students who were identified as being at-risk based on the universal screening data prior to referring on to Tier 2).
Who:	Ex. Instruction/Interventions provided by the general education teacher Specify:
What:	Ex. Core Curriculum, Visual/Verbal Cueing, Differentiation, etc. Specify:
Where:	Ex. General Education Classroom Specify:
How:	Ex. 90 minutes of core instruction(research-based) in targeted area daily Specify:
Time:	Ex. Minimum of 6 weeks Specify:
Assessment:	Ex. Progress monitoring occurs at least weekly for a minimum of 6 weeks or more after being identified at-risk based on the universal screening data Specify:
Description of the Problem:	
Student's Current Performance Level:	
Tier 1 Instruction/ Intervention Goal:	
Instruction/ Intervention Options:	• Option 1: • Option 2: • Option 3:
Instruction/ Intervention Implemented,	• Name & brief description of selected instruction/intervention:

Evaluation Criteria, & Dates, How, Frequency, and Duration of Implementation (ex. 6 weeks or more; 90 minutes of core instruction daily, targeted and specific differentiation, small group, graphic organizers):	• Implementation date & ending date: • How was the instruction/intervention implemented: • Duration & frequency of intervention/instruction (ex. number of weeks, number of days per week, number of minutes per day):
Person(s) Responsible for Implementing Instruction/ Intervention, Title, Name of Intervention, Length of Intervention, and Location of Services, and Follow-Up Date(s):	• Name: • Title: • Location: • Name of Intervention: • Length of Intervention: • Location of Service: • Follow-Up Date(s):
Fidelity & Validity Statement:	• I certify that the above-referenced Tier 1 intervention/instruction/strategies were implemented consistently and reliably as described. _____ Signature, Title, & Date of Person(s) Responsible for Implementing Tier 1 Instruction/Intervention
Progress Monitoring Data & Results:	• Performance Level: • Rate of Growth: • Evaluation Criteria:
Team Decision & Explanation for Tier 1:	❑ Tier 1 instruction/intervention successful ❑ Problem has not been resolved but progress is being made – continue with Tier 1 instruction/intervention/strategies ❑ Problem not resolved MODIFY Tier 1 instruction/intervention/strategies ❑ Problem not resolved CHANGE Tier 1 instruction/intervention/strategies to: _____ ❑ Problem not resolved performance level and/or rate of growth remain below acceptable levels – initiate Tier 2 instruction/intervention ❑ Brief Explanation of Team Decision:

ABC's for RTI & Behavior
Differentiated Instruction Lesson Plan Framework

Teacher:	Date(s):	Grade:	Subject:
Unit:	Assignment:	Materials:	Homework:

Unit/Concept Planning:			
Standard (content):			
Big Idea:			
Essential Question(s):			
Objective(s):			
Backward Design	Step 1: Identify Desired Results – Performance Tasks	Step 2: Determine Acceptable Evidence – Formative & Summative Assessment (product)	Step 3: Planned Learning Experiences & Instruction Demonstrating at Least 2 Facets of Understanding (explanation, interpretation, application, perspective, empathy, self-knowledge)
All			
Some – list students:			
Few (Struggling) – list students:			
Few (Advanced) – list students:			

Bloom's Taxonomy

Knowledge:	Comprehension:	Application:
list, define, tell, describe, identify, show, label, collect, examine, tabulate, quote, name, who, when, where, etc.	summarize, describe, interpret, contrast, predict, associate, distinguish, estimate, differentiate, discuss, extend, etc.	apply, demonstrate, calculate, complete, illustrate, show, examine, modify, relate, change, classify, experiment, discover, etc.
Analysis:	Synthesis:	Evaluation:
analyze, separate, order, explain, connect, classify, arrange, divide, compare, select, explain, infer, etc.	combine, integrate, modify, rearrange, substitute, plan, create, design, invent, prepare, generalize, rewrite, etc.	assess, decide, rank, grade, test, measure, recommend, convince, select, judge, explain, discriminate, support, conclude, compare, summarize, etc.

Elementary Interest Inventory (Grades 1-5)

Name: _____   Date: _____
Age & Grade: _____   School: _____

Directions: I want to get to know you better. Answer the following questions below and tell me what your likes and dislikes are.

1. Are you a boy or girl? _____

2. Do you like school?_____ Why or Why not? _____

3. What subject(s) do you like best in school? _____

4. What subject(s) do you like least in school? _____
5. Do you like to play sports? _____

    What sports do you like to play? _____

6. If you don't like sports, what do you like to do for fun?

    _____

7. Do you like to play/work on the computer? _____

    If so, what activities are your favorite when playing/working on the computer?

    _____

8. What do you do when you're at home? _____

9. Do you like to watch TV?_____

    What is/are your favorite TV show(s)?
    _____

10. Do you like to listen to music?_____ Who is your favorite group?_____

11. What is/are your favorite food(s)? _____

    What is/are your favorite restaurant(s)? _____

12. Do you like to go to the movies? _____ What kind of movies do you like? _____

13. What do you like to do with your friends after school?

    _____

14. What do you like to do on the weekend? _____

    _____

15. What do you like to do with your family? _____

    _____

16. If you had a million dollars, what would you do with it?

1st choice? _____

2nd choice? _____

3rd choice?_____

17. Tell me about other things you "like" and "dislike" about school or at home.

_____

_____

_____

_____

_____

_____

_____

Secondary Interest Inventory (Grades 6-12)

Name: _____ Date: _____

Age & Grade: _____ School: _____

Teacher: _____

Directions: I want to get to know you better. Answer the following questions below and tell me what your likes and dislikes are.

1. Are you male/female?_____

2. What is/are your favorite subject(s) in school? Tell me why.

_____

_____

3. What is/are your least favorite subject(s) in school? Tell me why.

_____

_____

4. What clubs/activities do you belong to in school or outside of school? If none, which ones would you like to belong to?

_____

5. What sports do you play in school or outside of school?

_____

6. If you like sports, what sport(s) is/are your favorite? _____

7. Who is/are your favorite sports team(s)? _____

   Who is/are your favorite athlete(s)? _____

8. If you don't like sports, what kinds of things do you like to do?

_____

_____

_____

9. What do you like to do after school? _____

10. What do you like to do in the evenings? _____

11. What do you like to do on the weekends? _____

12. Do you like to read?_____ If so, what are some of your favorite books? _____

13. What are some of your favorite T.V. shows? _____

14. What type of movies do you like?_____

    What is/are your favorite movie(s)?_____

    How often do you go to the movies?_____

    Who do you usually go with (family or friends)?_____

15. Where do you like to go with your friends?_____

    How often do you go out with your friends? _____

16. Do you drive?_____

    Do you have your own car?_____

    What type of car do you drive? _____

    What is your ideal car? _____

17. What are your hobbies? _____

18. What is your favorite kind of music? _____

19. What is/are your favorite song(s)?_____

20. Do you have a part-time job?_____ If yes, what do you do?_____

21. What do you want to do after you graduate from High School? _____

    _____

22. What do you hope to be doing five years after High School?

    _____

23. What type of job do you think you want after High School? _____

24. If you could be granted 3 wishes what would they be?

    1. _____

    2. _____

    3. _____

Behavioral Universal Screening
Total Classroom Performance Calculations

Teachers' Name: _____

Grade Level: _____

Name of School & System: _____

Circle Type of Class: General   Co-Taught/Inclusion   Special   Other:

Directions: Operationally define behavior expectations in observable and measurable terms for acceptable behavior, borderline behavior, and concerned behavior. Identify the students in need of additional supports (Tier 2 & Tier 3) and provide supports to those students. Chart school wide or class wide progress here over the school year. Individual student progress will be charted separately. Use this data to progress monitor behavioral performance.

Acceptable: _____

Borderline: _____

Concerned: _____

	Acceptable Range	Borderline Range	Concerned Range	Total % Increase / Decrease
Fall (Aug. – Oct.)	Total Number of Students in the Acceptable Range / Total Number of Students Assessed = _____ %	Total Number of Students in the Borderline Range / Total Number of Students Assessed = _____ %	Total Number of Students in Concerned Range / Total Number of Students Assessed = _____ %	
Winter (Nov. – Jan.)	Total Number of Students in the Acceptable Range / Total Number of Students Assessed = _____ %	Total Number of Students in the Borderline Range / Total Number of Students Assessed = _____ %	Total Number of Students in Concerned Range / Total Number of Students Assessed = _____ %	
Spring (Feb. – April)	Total Number of Students in the Acceptable Range / Total Number of Students Assessed = _____ %	Total Number of Students in the Borderline Range / Total Number of Students Assessed = _____ %	Total Number of Students in Concerned Range / Total Number of Students Assessed = _____ %	

Chapter 5
SELECTING AN INTERVENTION

Now that you've finally completed the universal screenings and have identified students in need of Tier 2 interventions here comes the hard part, knowing which intervention to implement and how long it should be implemented. Just in case you didn't know this, there is no list of scientifically validated reading, math, or behavior programs generated by the U.S. Department of Education. Therefore, you must do your homework and find out which interventions are research-based, best practice, or just packaged nicely. However, the U.S. Public Health Service has developed a classification system of approaches to prevent problem behavior. This system has coordinated and integrated a range of interventions to address the needs of the three types of students that are present in different proportions in every school: primary, secondary, and tertiary (Sprague, Cook, Wright, & Sadler, 2007).

From a practitioner's viewpoint, it is important to know and understand this classification system and use it to help develop appropriate interventions for students with diverse needs. I suggest educators begin with identifying a student's area of deficit and match an appropriate corresponding intervention to that deficit and then determine if the intervention is research based unless you're blessed with someone else providing you with this valuable information.

Now you must ask what constitutes a "research-based" intervention. In general, a research-based intervention consists of a set of practices that are tested and are evaluated in a controlled study by experts in the field and have appeared in peer reviewed journals. Students are matched according to the criteria of the study and are randomly assigned to a treatment or no treatment group. The outcomes of the students in both groups are compared and each intervention must be shown to be effective.

For educators to be effective it is important that they understand how to teach the standards, know how to differentiate, and know all the instructional interventions available in the building. This is important so both administrators and teachers can ensure that the core instruction and more intensive interventions are integrated across all tiers. If the general education classroom teacher does not know the nature and extent of the curriculum strategies used in supplemental or intensive instruction, then that teacher will be unable to integrate the supplemental/intensive instruction into the general education classroom. Likewise, if the teachers providing supplemental and intensive instruction are not aware of the task demands of the core instruction, it is likely that the supplemental and/or intensive instruction will be inconsistent and difficult for the student to use in the general education classroom. According to Gresham (2004), evidence based practices are to be used in three ways:

1. For selecting interventions
2. For evaluating the effectiveness of an intervention and
3. For assessing the degree of fidelity with which it is applied

Any discussion regarding the selection of an intervention must be accompanied by the discussion of fidelity/treatment integrity. Treatment fidelity is the degree in which something is implemented in the manner in which it was intended, designed, and planned. Fidelity can be measured by direct or indirect assessments. Direct assessment of treatment fidelity can be based on systematic observation of treatment implementation, task analysis of major treatment components, occurrence and nonoccurrence of each component implemented and recorded, or by level of integrity calculated by computed percentage of components implemented. Indirect assessment of treatment integrity can be measured by self-reports, interviews, or behavior ratings by observers. If interventions are not implemented with fidelity, then no accurate conclusions can be made about a student's responsiveness to intervention and its effectiveness because the intervention was not implemented as intended.

As previously noted, there is no comprehensive list of research-based validated curricula for reading, math, or behavior available as of today. But there is some information that is available, useful, and effective that can serve as a starting point for locating and selecting research validated interventions. This list is not intended to be an exhaustive list but a useful and practical list for educational practitioners.

READING INTERVENTIONS

The Florida Center for Reading Research (FCRR)

The *Florida Center for Reading Research* was established by Governor Jeb Bush in January, 2002. The center conducts basic research on reading, reading growth, reading assessment, and reading instruction that will contribute to the scientific knowledge of reading. The *Florida Center for Reading Research* disseminates information about research-based practices related to literacy instruction and assessment for children in pre-school through 12th grade. Extensive information on tiered research-based reading interventions for all students including struggling readers can be downloaded from their website for free at: http://www.fcrr.org/index.htm. Free downloads include: webcasts, podcasts, presentations, publications, assessment and progress monitoring tools, differentiated reading instruction lesson structures, reading center activities, principal reading walk-through checklist, interventions for struggling students, and much more.

National Reading Panel (NRP)

In 1997, Congress asked the Director of the *National Institute of Child Health and Human Development (NICHD),* along with the Secretary of Education, to convene a national panel on reading. The *National Reading Panel (NRP)* was asked by Congress to assess the status of research-based knowledge about reading, including the effectiveness of various approaches to teaching children to read. The panel was made up of 14 people, including leading scientists in reading research, representatives of colleges of education, teachers, educational administrators, and parents. The *NRP* met over a period of two years to discuss their findings and prepare the results in two reports and a video titled, *"Teaching Children to Read."*

Since the completion of this comprehensive report on reading assessment and instructional reading approaches, many organizations are turning to the NRP Report to highlight important findings that impact specific audiences such as parents, teachers, and school administrators in creating tools that will enable individuals to learn to read. Extensive information on how to teach reading can be downloaded from their website for free at: http://www.nationalreadingpanel.org/default.htm. Free downloads include: videos and publications inclusive of:

- *Putting Reading First: The Research Building Blocks for Teaching Children to Learn to Read Kindergarten Through Grade 3*
- *Put Reading First: Helping Your Child Learn to Read A Parent Guide Kindergarten Through Grade 3*

BIG IDEAS IN READING (University of Oregon)

Big Ideas in Beginning Reading focuses on the five big ideas of early literacy: phonemic awareness, alphabetic principle, fluency with text, vocabulary, and comprehension. The *Big Ideas in Beginning Reading* website is designed to provide information, technology, and resources to teachers, administrators, and parents across the country. It includes definitions and descriptions of the research and theories behind each of the big ideas, describes how to assess the big ideas, gives information on how to teach the big ideas including instructional examples, and finally, shows you how to put it all together in your school. The website can be accessed at: http://reading.uoregon.edu/index.php. Free downloads include: video clips, presentations, the Oregon Reading First Center: Review of Comprehensive Reading Programs document, the Oregon Reading First Center: Review of Supplemental and Intervention Programs document, information on how to select and evaluate a core reading program, models of reading program implementation, and much more.

The University of Oregon emphasizes that the purpose in releasing these reports is to provide a thorough and objective analysis of comprehensive programs in beginning reading for Oregon Reading First schools to use in their selection of a school-wide reading program in Grades K-3. The report is NOT:

- An approved or recommended reading textbook or program adoption list for Oregon or any other state;
- An endorsement of any specific program;
- An all-inclusive list of comprehensive reading programs in K-3. Only those publishers who submitted materials for review, and only those programs that met the criteria used in Oregon to define a comprehensive beginning reading program, were reviewed.

54

DIBELS Benchmark Goals and Indicators of Risk
Three Assessment Periods Per Year

Kindergarten

DIBELS Measure	Beginning of Year Month 1 - 3		Middle of Year Month 4 – 6		End of Year Month 7 - 10	
	Scores	Status	Scores	Status	Scores	Status
DIBELS Initial Sound Fluency	ISF < 4 4 <= ISF < 8 ISF >= 8	At risk Some risk Low risk	ISF < 10 10 <= ISF < 25 ISF >= 25	Deficit Emerging Established		
DIBELS Letter Naming Fluency	LNF < 2 2 <= LNF < 8 LNF >= 8	At risk Some risk Low risk	LNF < 15 15 <= LNF < 27 LNF >= 27	At risk Some risk Low risk	LNF < 29 29 <= LNF < 40 LNF >= 40	At risk Some risk Low risk
DIBELS Phoneme Segmentation Fluency			PSF < 7 7 <= PSF < 18 PSF >= 18	At risk Some risk Low risk	PSF < 10 10<= PSF < 35 PSF >= 35	Deficit Emerging Established
DIBELS Nonsense Word Fluency			NWF < 5 5 <= NWF < 13 NWF >= 13	At risk Some risk Low risk	NWF < 15 15 <= NWF < 25 NWF >= 25	At risk Some Risk Low risk

https://dibels.uoregon.edu/benchmark.php

DIBELS Benchmark Goals and Indicators of Risk
Three Assessment Periods Per Year

First Grade

DIBELS Measure	Beginning of Year Month 1 - 3		Middle of Year Month 4 – 6		End of Year Month 7 - 10	
	Scores	Status	Scores	Status	Scores	Status
DIBELS Letter Naming Fluency	LNF < 25 25 <= LNF < 37 LNF >= 37	At risk Some risk Low risk				
DIBELS Phoneme Segmentation Fluency	PSF < 10 10 <= PSF < 35 PSF >= 35	Deficit Emerging Established	PSF < 10 10 <= PSF < 35 PSF >= 35	Deficit Emerging Established	PSF < 10 10<= PSF < 35 PSF >= 35	Deficit Emerging Established
DIBELS Nonsense Word Fluency	NWF < 13 13 <= NWF > 24 NWF>= 24	At risk Some risk Low Risk	NWF < 30 30 <= NWF < 50 NWF >= 50	Deficit Emerging Established	NWF < 30 30 <= NWF < 50 NWF >= 50	Deficit Emerging Established
DIBELS Oral Reading Fluency			ORF < 8 8 <= ORF < 20 ORF >= 20	At risk Some risk Low risk	ORF < 20 20 <= ORF < 40 ORF >= 40	At risk Some risk Low risk

https://dibels.uoregon.edu/benchmark.php

DIBELS Benchmark Goals and Indicators of Risk
Three Assessment Periods Per Year

Second Grade

DIBELS Measure	Beginning of Year Month 1 - 3		Middle of Year Month 4 – 6		End of Year Month 7 - 10	
	Scores	Status	Scores	Status	Scores	Status
DIBELS Nonsense Word Fluency	NWF < 30 30 <= NWF > 50 NWF >= 50	Deficit Emerging Established				
DIBELS Oral Reading Fluency	ORF < 26 26 <= ORF < 44 ORF >= 44	At risk Some risk Low risk	ORF < 52 52 <= ORF < 68 ORF >= 68	At risk Some risk Low risk	ORF < 70 70 <= ORF < 90 ORF >= 90	At risk Some risk Low risk

Third Grade

DIBELS Measure	Beginning of Year Month 1 - 3		Middle of Year Month 4 – 6		End of Year Month 7 - 10	
	Scores	Status	Scores	Status	Scores	Status
DIBELS Oral Reading Fluency	ORF < 53 53 <= ORF < 77 ORF >= 77	At risk Some risk Low risk	ORF < 67 67 <= ORF < 92 ORF >= 92	At risk Some risk Low risk	ORF < 80 80 <= ORF < 110 ORF >= 110	At risk Some risk Low risk

https://dibels.uoregon.edu/benchmark.php

DIBELS Benchmark Goals and Indicators of Risk
Three Assessment Periods Per Year

Fourth Grade – Preliminary estimates based on Fuchs et al. (1993) and Hasbrouck & Tindal (1992). Odds not available.

DIBELS Measure	Beginning of Year Month 1 - 3		Middle of Year Month 4 – 6		End of Year Month 7 - 10	
	Scores	Status	Scores	Status	Scores	Status
DIBELS Oral Reading Fluency	ORF < 71	At risk	ORF < 83	At risk	ORF < 96	At risk
	71 <= ORF < 93	Some risk	83 <= ORF < 105	Some risk	96 <= ORF < 118	Some risk
	ORF > = 93	Low risk	ORF > = 105	Low risk	ORF > = 118	Low risk

Fifth Grade – Preliminary estimates based on Fuchs et al. (1993) and Hasbrouck & Tindal (1992). Odds not available.

DIBELS Measure	Beginning of Year Month 1 - 3		Middle of Year Month 4 – 6		End of Year Month 7 - 10	
	Scores	Status	Scores	Status	Scores	Status
DIBELS Oral Reading Fluency	ORF < 81	At risk	ORF < 94	At risk	ORF < 103	At risk
	81 <= ORF < 104	Some risk	94 <= ORF < 115	Some risk	103 <= ORF < 124	Some risk
	ORF > = 104	Low risk	ORF > = 115	Low risk	ORF > = 124	Low risk

Sixth Grade – Preliminary estimates based on Fuchs et al. (1993) and Hasbrouck & Tindal (1992). Odds not available.

DIBELS Measure	Beginning of Year Month 1 - 3		Middle of Year Month 4 – 6		End of Year Month 7 - 10	
	Scores	Status	Scores	Status	Scores	Status
DIBELS Oral Reading Fluency	ORF < 83	At risk	ORF < 99	At risk	ORF < 104	At risk
	83 <= ORF < 109	Some risk	99 <= ORF < 120	Some risk	104 <= ORF < 125	Some risk
	ORF >= 109	Low risk	ORF >= 120	Low risk	ORF >= 125	Low risk

https://dibels.uoregon.edu/benchmark.php

DIBELS Risk Level Chart – Grades 4-5

	Grade 4			Grade 5			
	Fall Assessment 1	Winter Assessment 2	Spring Assessment 3	Fall Assessment 1	Winter Assessment 2	Spring Assessment 3	
Oral Reading Fluency	0 – 70	0 – 82	0 – 95	0 – 80	0 – 93	0 – 102	HR
	71 – 92	83 – 104	96 – 117	81 – 103	94 – 114	103 – 123	MR
	93+	105+	118+	104+	115+	124+	LR

HR – High Risk: Seriously below grade level and in need of substantial intervention

MR – Medium Risk: Moderately below grade level and I need of substantial intervention

LR – Low Risk: At grade level

Note: Preliminary estimates based on Fuchs et al. (1993) and Hasbrouck & Tindal (1982). Odds not available.

https://dibels.uoregon.edu/benchmark.php

DIBELS Risk Levels Chart

	Kindergarten			First			Second			Third		
	Fall	Winter	Spring	Fall	Winter	Spring	Fall	Winter	Spring	Fall	Winter	Spring
	1	2	3	1	2	3	1	2	3	1	2	3
Initial Sounds Fluency	0-3	0-9	HR									
	4-7	10-24	MR									
	8-11	25-33	LR									
	12+	34+	AA									
Letter Naming Fluency	0-1	0-14	0-28	0-24	HR							
	2-7	15-26	29-39	25-36	MR							
	8-16	27-35	40-49	37-46	LR							
	17+	36+	50+	47+	AA							
Phoneme Segmentation Fluency		0-6	0-9	0-9	0-9	0-9	HR					
		7-17	10-34	10-34	10-34	10-34	MR					
		18-33	35-47	35-41	35-49	35-54	LR					
		34+	48+	42+	50+	55+	AA					
Nonsense Word Fluency		0-4	0-14	0-12	0-29	0-29	0-29	0-29	0-29	HR		
		5-12	15-24	13-23	30-49	30-49	30-49	30-49	30-49	MR		
		13-21	25-34	24-31	50-54	50-71	50-71	50-71	50-71	LR		
		22+	35+	32+	55+	72+	72+	72+	72+	AA		
Oral Reading Fluency			HR	0-1	0-7	0-19	0-25	0-51	0-69	0-52	0-66	0-79
			MR	2-6	8-19	20-39	26-43	52-67	70-89	53-76	67-91	80-109
			LR	7+	20-33	40-64	44-65	68-89	90-108	77-96	92-109	110-128
			AA	NA	34+	65+	66+	90+	109+	97+	110+	129+

HR – High Risk: Seriously below grade level and in need of substantial intervention
MR – Moderate Risk: Moderately below grade level and in need of additional intervention
LR – Low Risk: At grade level
AA – Above Average: At or above the 60th percentile

   Effective: July 2006
   Revised: 09/05/2006

Note: Pending future research, ORF Fall assessment in first grade is not color-coded on this chart as an indication of risk status. Estimated levels of risk will be identified within the PMRN, however.
https://dibels.uoregon.edu/benchmark.php

Oregon Reading First Center: Review of Comprehensive Reading First Programs
(Individual Programs)

Program Name:	Publisher:
Houghton Mifflin's The Nation's Choice	Houghton Mifflin
Macmillan/McGraw-Hill Reading 2003	Macmillan/McGraw-Hill
Open Court	SRA
Reading Mastery Plus	SRA/McGraw-Hill
Rigby Literacy	Harcourt Rigby
Scott Foresman Reading	Scott Foresman
Success For All	Success For All Foundation
Trophies	Harcourt
Wright Group Literacy	Wright Group/McGraw-Hill

Useful Reading Intervention Websites:

Intervention Central	www.interventioncentral.org
Florida Center for Reading Research	http://www.fcrr.org/
National Reading Panel	http://www.nationalreadingpanel.org/default.htm
The Access Center	http://www.k8accesscenter.org/index.php
What Works Clearninghouse: Beginning Reading	http://ies.ed.gov/ncee/wwc/reports/topic.aspx?tid=01
Peer Assisted Learning Strategies (PALS)	http://kc.vanderbilt.edu/pals/teachmat/default.html
Best Evidence Encyclopedia Center for Data Driven Reform in Education	http://www.bestevidence.org/index.htm
Read, Write, Think	http://www.readwritethink.org/
Dynamic Indicators of Basic Early Literacy Skills	http://dibels.uoregon.edu/
Starfall	http://www.starfall.com/

MATH INTERVENTIONS

In 2006, President Bush and U.S. Secretary of Education Margaret Spellings announced a panelist of experts who were chosen to comprise the National Mathematics Advisory Panel (NMP). The panel advised President Bush and Secretary Spellings on the best use of scientifically based research to advance the teaching and learning of mathematics. The panel declared that mathematics education in the United States is broken and all schools need to focus on ensuring that all children master fundamental skills that provide the underpinnings for success in higher math.

The *National Mathematics Advisory Panel* modeled after the *National Reading Panel*, was created to examine and summarize scientific evidence related to the teaching and learning of mathematics, with a specific focus on preparation for and success in learning algebra. March 2008, the NMP presented: *The Foundations for Success: The Final Report of the National Mathematics Advisory Panel* to President Bush and Secretary Spellings. Here is a summary report of those findings and recommendations:

Math Benchmarks for the Critical Foundations

Fluency With Whole Numbers:
• By the end of grade 3, students should be proficient with the addition and subtraction of whole numbers. • By the end of grade 5, students should be proficient with multiplication and division of whole numbers.
Fluency With Fractions:
• By the end of grade 4, students should be able to identify and represent fractions and decimals, and compare them on a number line or with other common representation of fractions and decimals. • By the end of grade 5, students should be proficient with comparing fractions and decimals and common percent, and with the addition and subtraction of fractions and decimals. • By the end of grade 6, students should be proficient with multiplication and division of fractions and decimals. • By the end of grade 6, students should be proficient with all operations involving positive and negative integers. • By the end of grade 7, students should be proficient with all operations involving positive and negative fractions. • By the end of grade 7, students should be able to solve problems involving percent, ratio, and rate, and extend this work to proportionality.
Geometry and Measurement:
• By the end of grade 5, students should be able to solve problems involving perimeter and area of triangles and all quadrilaterals having at least one pair of parallel sides (i.e., trapezoids). • By the end of grade 6, students should be able to analyze the properties of two-dimensional shapes and solve problems involving perimeter and area, and analyze the properties of three-dimensional shapes and solve problems involving surface area and volume. • By the end of grade 7, students should be familiar with the relationship between similar triangles and the concept of the slope of a line.
Recommendation: The benchmarks for the critical foundations should be used to guide classroom curricula, mathematics instruction, and state assessments. They should be interpreted flexibly, to allow for the needs of students and teachers.

National Mathematics Advisory Panel 2008

The Major Topics of School Algebra

Symbols and Expressions:
• Polynomial expressions • Rational expressions • Arithmetic and finite geometric series
Linear Equations:
• Real numbers as points on the number line • Linear equations and their graphs • Solving problems with linear equations • Linear inequalities and their graphs • Graphing and solving systems of simultaneous linear equations
Quadratic Equations:
• Factors and factoring of quadratic polynomials with integer coefficients • Completing the square in quadratic expressions • Quadratic formula and factoring of general quadratic polynomials • Using the quadratic formula to solve equations
Functions:
• Linear functions • Quadratic functions – word problems involving quadratic functions • Graphs of quadratic functions and completing the square • Polynomial functions (including graphs of basic functions) • Simple nonlinear functions (e.g., square and cube root functions; absolute value; rational functions; step functions) • Rational exponents, radical expressions, and exponential functions • Logarithmic functions • Trigonometric functions • Fitting simple mathematical models to data
Algebra of Polynomials:
• Roots and factorization of polynomials • Complex numbers and operations • Fundamental theorem of algebra • Binomial coefficients (and Pascal's Triangle) • Mathematical induction and the binomial theorem
Combinatorics and Finite Probability:
• Combinations and permutations, as applications of the binomial theorem and Pascal's Triangle
Recommendation #1: The Panel recommends that school algebra be consistently understood in the terms of the Major Topics of School Algebra Recommendation #2: The Major Topics of School Algebra, accompanied by a thorough elucidation of the mathematical connections among these topics, should be the focus of Algebra I and Algebra II standards in the state curriculum frameworks in Algebra I and Algebra II courses, in textbooks for integrated curricula or otherwise, and in end of curse assessments of these two levels of Algebra.

National Mathematics Advisory Panel 2008

Key recommendations from the 2008 National Mathematics Advisory Panel Final Report indicate:

- The benchmarks for the critical foundations should be used to guide classroom curricula, mathematics instruction, and state assessments and they should be interpreted flexibly, to allow for the needs of students and teachers.
- The Panel recommends that school algebra be consistently understood in the terms of the Major Topics of School Algebra.

- The Major Topics of School Algebra, accompanied by a thorough elucidation of the mathematical connections among these topics, should be the focus of Algebra I and Algebra II standards in the state curriculum frameworks in Algebra I and Algebra II courses, in textbooks for integrated curricula or otherwise, and in end of course assessments of these two levels of Algebra.

A complete copy of *The Foundations for Success: The Final Report of the National Mathematics Advisory Panel* 2008 can be located at: http://www.ed.gov/about/bdscomm/list/mathpanel/index.html. These findings should guide grade level math interventions in the tiered Response to Intervention Process.

Following are useful math intervention websites that will assist you with some free to low cost math interventions for your students. Many of the websites provide interactive math support for your students while others provide research, guidance, information on math intervention strategies, lesson plans, PowerPoints, math tutorials, math games, etc.

Useful Math Intervention Websites:

Intervention Central	www.interventioncentral.org
Peer Assisted Learning Strategies (PALS)	http://kc.vanderbilt.edu/pals/teachmat/default.html
Best Evidence Encyclopedia Center for Data Driven Reform in Education	http://www.bestevidence.org/index.htm
The Video Math Tutor	http://www.videomathtutor.com/
Otter Creek Institute	http://www.oci-sems.com/Products/ProductLine.aspx?cat=501
Tutor Next	http://www.tutornext.com/
MathDrills.com	http://www.mathdrills.com/
The Access Center	http://www.k8accesscenter.org/index.php
What Works Clearninghouse: Elementary Math	http://ies.ed.gov/ncee/wwc/reports/topic.aspx?tid=04
What Works Clearninghouse: Middle School Math	http://ies.ed.gov/ncee/wwc/reports/topic.aspx?tid=03
Connected Mathematics	http://connectedmath.msu.edu/
Everyday Mathematics	http://everydaymath.uchicago.edu/
APlus Math	http://www.aplusmath.com/
Cook Math 4 Kids	http://www.coolmath4kids.com/
Edinformatives	http://www.edinformatics.com/kids_teens/kt_math.htm
Figure This Math Challenges for Families	http://www.figurethis.org/index.html
The Math Forum at Drexel	http://mathforum.org/arithmetic/arith.software.html
National Library of Virtual Manipulatives	http://nlvm.usu.edu/
Math Video Instructional Development Source	http://coe.jmu.edu/mathvids2/

BEHAVIORS INTERVENTIONS

"To be or not to be, that is the question…"

This famous phrase first coined in the 1600's by William Shakespeare in the play *Hamlet* seems fitting for teachers who now ask, "academics or behavior, that is the question". Educators find it difficult to focus on both academics and behavior mainly because of the pressure to focus on academics brought about by the federal mandate of *No Child Left Behind (NCLB)* that requires all students to be 100% proficient by 2014. Educators recognize the importance of focusing on academics and behavior, but since teachers are primarily measured by their students' academic performance, improving social and behavioral competence of students is low on the totem pole of urgency until a dangerous, litigiousness, or compliance related issue escalates. This is unfortunate, but often true.

As you already know, RTI is a multi-tiered proactive approach designed to help struggling learners succeed before they fail. Students' academic progress is closely monitored to determine the need for further instruction, but many educators have neglected to assess and progress monitor problem behavior of students in need of more intensive behavioral supports which presents a significant risk to the loss of precious instructional time. This loss of instructional time is not only detrimental to the students themselves with behavioral challenges, but it is also detrimental to all other students, teachers, and staff in the schools with them. It is extremely important that educators be reminded of the importance of "research to practice" and its implication on improving student achievement. In a study conducted by Hawkins, Catalano, Kosterman, Abbott, & Hill (1999), research findings indicate that if schools raise their academic achievement, behavior problems decrease and conversely when schools work to decrease behavior problems, students' academics improve.

The question of academics or behavior also poses another interesting question, which comes first the chicken or the egg? Or better yet, which comes first, behavior problems or academic problems? Who knows, but due to this common overlap of student problem behaviors and failing academics, most educators agree that it is rare to find a student who has behavior challenges who does not also have academic challenges, and often these behavioral problems start because of the student's inability to succeed academically at a level comparable to their peers. Dr. Joe Witt would then ask the question, is it a "can't-do" problem or a "won't-do" problem? This is an essential question to ask because the answer could directly impact the type and kind of behavioral intervention to use. A student with a "can't-do" problem is at-risk because they cannot complete an educational task because they don't have the prerequisite skills. A student with a "won't-do" problem is at-risk of failure because they have a motivation problem and choose not to complete a task. Even though both problems result in failure, the interventions used to address these problems may be different.

To further support this point, in an analysis conducted by the Florida Positive Behavior Support Project, three schools in Florida found that over 80% of all students identified as having severe behavioral problems were also identified by their teachers as having academic problems. Due to these findings, it is recommended that if a student has shown poor responsiveness to universal and classroom behavioral interventions, their academic proficiency should also be assessed. If the student has academic deficits, they should receive evidence-based interventions that directly address both their academic and behavioral needs. Schools may find that it is necessary to provide both academic and behavioral interventions simultaneously, but a judgment of the student's response to the behavioral interventions should be interpreted cautiously until the academic problems are remediated (University of South Florida Problem Solving and Response to Intervention Project, 2007).

With the passage of the *No Child Left Behind Act* and the revision of IDEA, schools are now looking at proactive approaches to address problem behaviors using the Response to Intervention problem solving model that matches intervention to students' level of need. When looking at RTI and behavior and the three-tiered model, Tier 1 (primary prevention) refers to the use of proactive intervention approaches that prevent problem behaviors from occurring. Tier 2 (secondary prevention) refers to addressing problems that already exist, but are not yet of a chronic nature or severe magnitude. These are used for students who did not respond to Tier 1 primary preventions. Tertiary prevention (Tier 3) interventions are used to address problem behaviors of students who are chronically at risk and did not respond to Tier 1 nor Tier 2 behavioral interventions.

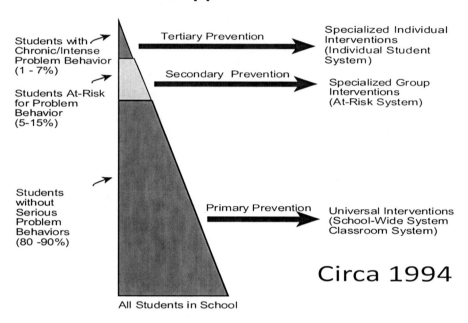

The OSEP National Technical Assistance Center on Positive Behavioral Interventions & Supports (www.pbis.org, 2007) provides capacity building information and technical support regarding behavioral and discipline systems needed for successful learning and social development of students. The Center also helps explain how to successfully implement RTI and tiered behavioral supports in schools. Positive Behavior Supports (PBS), like RTI is based on a problem-solving model that aims to prevent inappropriate behavior by teaching and reinforcing appropriate behaviors. Positive behavior supports provides, differentiated tiered interventions that are systematically applied to students based on their identified level of need and addresses the role environment plays in the development and improvement of behavior problems.

Extensive information on tiered research-based behavioral interventions can be located on the Center on Positive Behavioral Intervention & Supports website at: www.pbis.org. The website includes articles, webcasts, podcasts, presentations, etc.

Following are useful behavior intervention websites that will assist you with some free to low cost behavior intervention for use with your students exhibiting challenging behaviors. Websites include a variety of resources including examples of: classroom behavior management plans, behavior games, level systems, behavior contracts, functional behavioral assessments, behavior intervention plans, and much more.

Useful Behavior Intervention Websites:

Florida's Positive Behavior Support Project	http://flpbs.fmhi.usf.edu/index.asp
Intervention Central	www.interventioncentral.org
OSEP Technical Assistance Center on PBIS	www.pbis.org
Center for Evidence Based Practice: Young Children with Challenging Behavior	http://challengingbehavior.fmhi.usf.edu/
MODEL: Managing On-Site Discipline for Effective Learning	http://www.modelprogram.com/
Dr. Mac's Behavior Management Site	http://www.behavioradvisor.com/
What Works Clearinghouse	http://ies.ed.gov/ncee/wwc/
RTI Tools: A Response to Intervention Directory	http://www.rtitools.com/

Chapter 6

TIERS OF INTERVENTION AND THE IMPLEMENTATION PROCESS

RTI & Behavior: Tier 1 (Universal)

Response to Intervention and Positive Behavior Support (PBS) support a preventative approach to teaching academic and social behavior at Tier 1. The universal curriculum focuses on social skills all students are expected to exhibit which consist of consistent rules, expectations, and procedures which provide high quality school-wide behavioral instruction which helps to elevate behavioral curricula and instruction to levels of importance to that of academics. In PBS schools, the practice of teaching and reinforcing students for exhibiting school-wide expectations is considered to be a universal intervention, delivered to every student in every setting. By teaching and reinforcing expected behaviors, teachers and other professionals using PBS increase the probability that the majority of students will act according to the expectations, which acts as a proactive intervention for students with a history of challenging behaviors.

While the examination of office discipline referrals (ODRs) is necessary to identify students with high rates of externalizing behaviors, they are not sufficient for identifying all students in need of Tier 2 interventions. Students with internalizing behaviors are often not identified through ODR (Nelson, Bennen, Reid, & Epstein, 2002). The behavioral needs of these students must also be addressed to prevent problem behaviors from occurring in schools. Therefore schools must implement behavioral screenings that will help identify at-risk students who exhibit both internalizing and externalizing behaviors. However, to date, there is no such screening or identification measure that has been widely used or investigated within the behavioral model of RTI so data from office discipline referrals, absences, suspensions, expulsions, teacher nominations, grades, etc. have to be used to determine which students require additional supports. It is only after this data has been gathered along with high-quality academic and behavior instruction and interventions are established at both the school-wide and classroom levels that schools can determine that a student needs additional supports and needs to be referred on to Tier 2. (see Chapter 4 for step-by-step process and recommended forms for Tier 1).

RTI & Behavior: Tier 2 (Secondary Prevention)

For students identified in need of Tier 2 interventions, both RTI and PBS promote the use of research-based interventions tailored to students' level of identified need. Tier 2 interventions should be effective, easy to administer, and be appropriate for targeted small groups of students needing more intensive interventions than those received in Tier 1. Tier 1, like Tier 2 advocates for the use of evidenced- based interventions, that are implemented with fidelity, over a designated period of time, ex. 1 hour per week for 9 weeks, with progress monitoring, ex. 1 time per week (refer to your district/state level requirements for specific details). Students who are not successful at Tier 2 should be referred on to Tier 3.

Vaugh and Roberts (2007) have developed a general overview of multi-tiered interventions in the RTI model. However, it is important to remember that many States have adopted a three-tiered model of RTI implementation, but not all States have used this exact model so it's extremely important to note the differences between the three-tiered model and the model adopted by your State Department of Education.

Overview of Tiers

	Tier 1	Tiers 2 - 3	Tier 4
Definition	Instruction and programs, including ongoing professional development and benchmark assessments (3 times per year)	Instructional intervention employed to supplement, enhance, and support Tier 1; takes place in small groups	Individualized reading instruction extended beyond the time allocated for Tier 1; groups of 1-3 students
Focus	All students	Students identified with academic difficulties who have not responded to Tier 1 efforts	Student with marked difficulties with academics who have not responded adequately to Tier 1 or Tier 2-3 efforts.
Program	Scientifically based instruction and curriculum emphasizing the critical elements.	Specialized, scientifically based instruction and curriculum emphasizing the critical elements	Sustained, intensive, scientifically base instruction and curriculum highly responsive to students' needs.
Instruction	Sufficient opportunities to practice throughout the school day	• Additional attention, focus, support • Additional opportunities to practice embedded throughout the day • Pre-teach, review skill; frequent opportunities to practice skills	Carefully designed and implement, explicit, systematic instruction
Interventionist	General education teacher	Personnel determined by the school (classroom teacher, specialized reading teacher, specialized instructional teacher, other trained	Personnel determined by the school (e.g., specialized reading teacher, special education teacher)

		personnel)	
Setting	General education classroom	Appropriate setting designated by the school	Appropriate setting designated by the school
Grouping	Flexible grouping	Homogeneous small-group instruction (e.g., 1:4, 1:5)	Homogeneous small-group instruction
Time	Recommendation of 90 minutes per day	20-30 minutes per day in addition to Tier 1	50-min sessions (or longer) per day depending upon appropriateness of Tier 1
Assessment	Benchmark assessments at the beginning, middle, and end of academic year	Progress monitoring twice a month on target skill to ensure adequate progress and learning	Progress monitoring at least twice per month on target skill to ensure adequate progress and learning

Vaugh, S. & Roberts (2007)

Following is a table of step-by-step instructions for implementing RTI and behavior in Tier 2. This table is to be used as a guide for implementation along with sample data collection forms.

Steps in the RTI & Behavior Implementation Process
Tier 2

Tier 2	Tier 2 is provided to all at-risk students who did not respond to Tier 1 based on academic and/or behavioral performance. Interventions must occur within a small group (e.g. 3 to 5) within the general education classroom.
Focus of Tier 2	The focus of Tier 2 requires high-quality instruction matched to student need. Tier 2 occurs in addition to Tier 1. Tier 2 intervention recommend an additional 90 minutes per week of targeted instruction focused on the student's area(s) of identified need. Behavior deficits are to be addressed in conjunction with academic deficits. If a student is identified as being below the 25th percentile on a designated cut point in reading, math and/or behavior, a minimum of 120 minutes of targeted intervention is recommended. The additional 90 to 120 minutes of intervention must occur across a minimum of 2 sessions per week and the duration of each session should be appropriate to the age/grade level and development of the child. *(Note: The law speaks to the minimum required and is not necessarily the standard for best practice, or meeting the targeted needs of each student).*
Examples of data to be examined	Discipline/office referrals, attendance, tardies, suspensions, grades, test scores (formal & informal), juvenile justice records, family crisis (homelessness, divorce, death, unemployment, abuse, neglect, etc. – use professional judgment)
What happens at Tier 2	<ul><li>Tier 1 + Tier 2</li><li>Continue teaching core curriculum with fidelity</li><li>Secondary preventions/interventions are provided to at-risk students who did not respond to Tier 1 interventions using Standard Protocol and/or Problem Solving interventions</li><li>Supplemental social behavioral support is added to reduce the current number and intensity of problem behavior</li><li>Addresses problems that already exist but are not yet of a chronic nature or a severe magnitude</li><li>Interventions are more individualized than Tier 1</li><li>Differentiation is different and more individualized than Tier 1</li><li>Targeted interventions are developed for at-risk students</li><li>Use research-based, scientifically validated interventions and continue delivering core curriculum with fidelity</li><li>Develop a system for increasing structure and predictability</li><li>Develop a system for increasing contingent adult feedback</li><li>Develop a system for linking academic and behavioral</li></ul>

	performance • Develop a system for increasing home/school communication • Progress monitoring at-risk students in deficit areas (e.g. one time per week for 9 to 12 weeks) • Collect and use of data for instructional and behavioral decision-making • Teams use instructional and behavioral assessments to identify students not mastering behavioral skills at the same rate as peers • Students who continue to fall behind are identified for Tier 3 supports
Examples of Tier 2 Interventions	• Tier 1 + Tier 2 interventions • Check in check out • Targeted social skills instruction • Peer based supports • Social skills clubs • Planned discussions • Goal Setting • Anger management training • Behavior contracts based on information from student interest inventories • Positive reinforcement • Direct social skills instruction • Verbal and/or visual schedules • Cognitive behavior therapy • Self-monitoring/self-evaluation • Modeling • Visualizations • Self-talk • Teach desired behaviors
	Steps to Implementing Tier 2
Step 1	Identify students needing targeted group interventions/Tier 2 (e.g. those performing at or below the lowest 20%; or students performing at or below the 25th percentile on a screening measure; or students performing at or below a pre-determined cut score) from those meeting benchmark/Tier 1, etc.
Step 2	Determine and document how to best meet Tier 2 students' specific academic and/or behavioral needs with grade level or content level team members using the standard protocol and/or problem solving treatment model. Data source examples: attendance records, discipline records

	(e.g. suspension, expulsion, office referrals, non-compliance data, etc.), semester grades, results of curriculum based measurements (CBM), results of formal and/or informal assessments, formative assessments and/or summative assessments, etc.
Step 3	Determine person(s) responsible for implementing instruction/intervention, their title, type of intervention, length of intervention, and location of services.
Step 4	Provide research based, scientifically validated targeted interventions matched to student's need. Implement with fidelity. Remember intervention must occur for a minimum of 9 to 12 weeks with weekly progress monitoring.

Step 5	1. Chart data and begin with the initial scores received on the universal screening.
	2. Chart goal line and chart progress. Remember you need a minimum of 3 to 5 data points on a goal line to judge if progress is sufficient and further decision making can be determined.
	3. Chart end of the year benchmark/goal.
	4. Determine if intervention is successful based on a problem solving method, established benchmarks, learning rate and level of performance, and document team decision to continue, modify, or change intervention. Possible questions to consider:
	  a) Was the core curriculum and intervention delivered with fidelity?
	  b) Did the intervention match the student's specific area of need?
	  c) Was the teacher/ interventionist trained to deliver the intervention?
	  d) Did the student attend all scheduled sessions of the intervention?
	  e) Did the student receive differentiated needs-based instruction?
	  f) Is the student making progress?
	  g) Is the student making progress, but not yet on target to meet benchmark?
	  h) Does the student's performance differ greatly from his/her age/grade level peers?
	  i) Is the student not making sufficient progress to be on trajectory toward meeting benchmark(s)?
	  j) What strategies/interventions are needed to help this student make progress?

Step 6	• Identify students who were successful in Tier 2 and will return to Tier 1 • Identify students who are making adequate progress, but

	are not yet meeting benchmark(s) and will remain in Tier 2 • Identify students in need of Tier 3 interventions • Complete the Tier 2 Secondary Prevention Data Collection & Intervention Documentation Form • Review and complete as needed all other relevant Tier 2 recommended forms • Complete any other district or state level required documents for Tier 2

ABC's of Response to Intervention (RTI)
Data Collection & Intervention Documentation Forms

Student's Name: _____ Grade: _____
Date of Birth: _____ Student ID#: _____
School & District: _____ Homeroom Teacher: _____ Content: _____

	Tier 2 – Secondary Prevention (Targeted Group Interventions)
Who:	Ex. Instruction/Interventions provided by the general education teacher or other trained educational professionals Specify:
What:	Ex. Core Curriculum, Visual/Verbal Cueing, Differentiation, Direct Instruction, etc. Specify:
Where:	Ex. General Education Classroom Specify:
How:	Ex. 30 minutes of research-based supplemental instruction/interventions, 2 to 3 times per week in a small group (no more than 5 students) PLUS Tier 1 core instruction for 90 minutes per day in targeted areas Specify:
Time:	Ex. 9 to 12 weeks Specify:
Assessment:	Ex. Progress monitoring occurs 2 to 3 times per month for a minimum of 9 to 12 weeks Specify:
Description of the Problem:	
Student's Current Performance Level:	
Tier 2 Instruction/ Intervention Goal:	
Instruction/ Intervention Options:	• Option 1: • Option 2:

	• Option 3:
Instruction/ Intervention Implemented & Dates, How, Frequency, and Duration of Implementation (ex. 9 to 12 weeks; 30 minutes of supplemental instruction 3 times per week PLUS 90 minutes of core instruction in small group using differentiated instructional strategies):	• Name & brief description of selected instruction/intervention Option: • Implementation date & ending date: • How was the instruction/intervention implemented: • Duration & frequency of intervention/instruction (ex. number of weeks, number of days per week, number of minutes per day):
Person(s) Responsible for Implementing Instruction/ Intervention, Title, Name of Intervention, Length of Intervention, and Location of Services, and Follow-Up Date(s):	• Name: • Title: • Location: • Name of Intervention: • Length of Intervention: • Location of Service: • Follow-Up Date(s):
Fidelity & Validity Statement:	• I certify that the above referenced Tier 2 intervention/instruction was implemented consistently and reliably as described. _____ Signature, Title, & Date of Person(s) Responsible for Implementing Tier 2 Instruction/Intervention
Progress Monitoring Data & Results: (see progress monitoring graphs)	• Performance Level: • Rate of Growth: • Evaluation Criteria:
Team Decision & Explanation for Tier 2:	❑ Tier 2 instruction/intervention successful – exit Tier 2 and return to Tier 1 instruction/intervention ❑ Problem has not been resolved but progress is being made –

	continue with Tier 2 instruction/intervention
	❑ Problem not resolved MODIFY Tier 2 instruction/intervention
	❑ Problem not resolved CHANGE Tier 2 instruction/intervention to:
	_____
	❑ Problem not resolved performance level and/or rate of growth remain below acceptable levels – initiate Tier 3 instruction/intervention
	❑ Brief Explanation of Team Decision:

ABC's of Response to Intervention (RTI) and Behavior
Comprehensive At-Risk Student Questionnaire

Recommended: To ONLY be completed on students referred to Tier 2 or beyond (ex. Tier 3)

Directions: Complete each section below and answer all applicable questions as thoroughly as possible. You may not have all the answers to each of the questions. Some sections and questions are designed for teachers/educators serving the student to answer. Other sections and questions are designed for the student's parents/guardians to answer and some sections and questions are designed for teachers to ask students to answer. Try to complete each section and the related questions to the best of your ability. Some questions may be left unanswered if the team feels the questions are not applicable or are not appropriate. Some questions are more applicable when there is a suspicion that the child may have a disability. Always follow state and district guidelines in responding to any of the questions listed below. CONFIDENTIALITY and PROFESSIONAL JUDGEMENT SHOULD ALWAYS BE USED. Once the comprehensive student profile has been completed, review the answers within each section and use this information as a "guide" to help analyze and determine the types of instructional and/or behavioral supports and interventions needed to help the student improve academic and/or behavioral proficiencies.

I. Student Profile Information

Initial Request for Assistance (Date):

Reason for referral:

Student Name: Student ID: Social Security Number:

Student Address:

Student Home Telephone:

Date of Birth: Age: Gender: Race/Ethnicity: Origin:

Grade: Referring Teacher:

Diploma Track: College Prep   Tech Prep   GED   Special Education   Other:

School: School System: FTE:

School's Address:

    City:

    State/Province:

    Zip/Postal Code:

School Phone Number:

School Fax Number:

1. Is this student an English Language Learner/Bilingual Learner: Yes   No

    If yes, primary language: secondary language:

    If yes, are ESL/Bilingual services provided in school?   Yes   No

    If yes, how many hours per   Week?   Month?

2. What is the primary language of the English Language Learner Instructor?

    Secondary Language?

3.   Is this student a minority?   Yes   No

If yes, does this student's speech/language have a negative impact on their educational performance (academic or non-academic)?   Yes   No

4.   Has this student passed a vision screening? Yes (If yes, when):

No (if no – stop process until passed)

5.   Does this student wear glasses?   Yes   No

6.   Has this student passed a hearing screening? Yes (If yes, when):

No (if no – stop process until passed)

7.   Does this student wear hearing aids?   Yes   No

8.   Does this student have a psychological available for review? Yes   No

Don't Know

9.   Does this student have medical records available for review? Yes   No

Don't Know

10. Is this student on any daily medications?   Yes   No

If so, what, why, and dosage?

11. Is this student considered to have an environmental disadvantage? Yes   No

12. Is this student considered to be economically disadvantaged?   Yes   No

13. Does this student have an atypical educational history?   Yes   No

If yes, explain:

14.   Supplemental services received: Pre-K   Early Intervention   ESL   Title I Speech/Language, Other, None (Indicate hours per day, week, or month for each)

15. Has this student ever attended 2 or more schools in any school year(s)? Yes   No

If yes, which school year(s)?

16. Has the student ever been retained, administratively placed, or been socially promoted?

Yes   No   If yes, how many times?   If yes, what grade?

17. Has the student ever participated in any type of academic program such as a preschool program?

Yes   No   If yes, when (year) After-school program?

Educational Program?

Extended School Year Program?

18. Length of School Day: 6 hrs (standard) If other explain:

II. Educational Environment:

Location of Classes

Reading: General Education, Inclusion, Early Intervention, Resource, Self-Contained, Other

19. Language Arts: General Education, Inclusion, Early Intervention, Resource, ESL, Self-Contained, Other

20. Math: General Education, Inclusion, Early Intervention, Resource, Self-Contained, Other

21. Science: General Education, Inclusion, Early Intervention, Resource, Self-Contained, Other

22. Social Studies: General Education, Inclusion, Early Intervention, Resource, Self-Contained, Other

23. Other (Explain):

III. Attendance & Suspension:

24. Are there any years the student missed school for 5 or more school days in one year?

Yes   No

If yes, please list the year and the number of days:

If yes, which school year?   Did they receive any failing grades? If so, list.

25. Absences for Current & Previous Year:

(CY = Current Year, PY = Previous Year, Q1 = 1st Quarter, Q 2 = 2nd Quarter, etc.):

CY-Q1 =   CY-Q2 =   CY-Q3 =   CY-Q4 =

PY-Q1 =   PY-Q2 =   PY-Q3 =   PY-Q4 =

26. Out of School Suspensions (current year):
    CY-Q1 =   CY-Q2 =   CY-Q3 =   CY-Q4 =

    PY-Q1 =   PY-Q2 =   PY-Q3 =   PY-Q4 =

27. Reasons:
    CY-Q1 =   CY-Q2 =   CY-Q3 =   CY-Q4 =

    PY-Q1 =   PY-Q2 =   PY-Q3 =   PY-Q4 =

28. In School Suspensions (current year):
    CY-Q1 =   CY-Q2 =   CY-Q3 =   CY-Q4 =

    PY-Q1 =   PY-Q2 =   PY-Q3 =   PY-Q4 =

29. Reasons:
    CY-Q1 =   CY-Q2 =   CY-Q3 =   CY-Q4 =

    PY-Q1 =   PY-Q2 =   PY-Q3 =   PY-Q4 =

30. Is this student working on the appropriate age/grade level curriculum? Yes   No
    If yes, are research-based accommodations and modifications being used, if so list type
    of accommodation/modification, dates/timeframe used, and outcome?

V.   Grades:

Grades Current & Previous Year

(CY = Current Year, PY = Previous Year, Q1 = 1st Quarter, Q 2 = 2nd Quarter, etc.):

31. Reading:

CY-Q1 =   PY-Q1 =   CY-Q2 =   PY-Q2 =

CY-Q3 =   PY- Q3 =   CY-Q4 =   PY-Q4 =

Accommodations/modifications used? Yes   No   If yes, list:

Dates/Timeframe used:

Outcome:

32. Language Arts:

CY-Q1 =   PY-Q1 =   CY-Q2 =   PY-Q2 =

CY-Q3 =   PY- Q3 =   CY-Q4 =   PY-Q4 =

Accommodations/modifications used? Yes   No   If yes, list:

Dates/Timeframe used:

Outcome:

33. Math:

CY-Q1 =   PY-Q1 =   CY-Q2 =   PY-Q2 =

CY-Q3 =   PY- Q3 =   CY-Q4 =   PY-Q4 =

Accommodations/modifications used? Yes   No   If yes, list:

Dates/Timeframe used:

Outcome:

34. Science:

    CY-Q1 =   PY-Q1 =   CY-Q2 =   PY-Q2 =

     CY-Q3 =   PY- Q3 =   CY-Q4 =   PY-Q4 =

Accommodations/modifications used? Yes   No   If yes, list:

Dates/Timeframe used:

Outcome:

35. Social Studies:

     CY-Q1 =   PY-Q1 =   CY-Q2 =   PY-Q2 =

      CY-Q3 =   PY- Q3 =   CY-Q4 =   PY-Q4 =

Accommodations/modifications used? Yes   No   If yes, list:

Dates/Timeframe used:

Outcome:

V. Standardized Test Scores:

36. Assessment 1 (name of assessment):   Date of assessment:

Total Score: Scale Score: Passed   or   Failed
Domain Names & scores:

Domain A (name): _____	Domain B: (name): _____	Domain C: (name): _____	Domain D: (name): _____	Domain E: (name): _____	Domain F: (name): _____
Score: (# correct/ possible # of correct items: _____	Score: (# correct/ possible # of correct items: _____	Score: (# correct/ possible # of correct items: _____	Score: (# correct/ possible # of correct items: _____	Score: (# correct/ possible # of correct items: _____	Score: (# correct/ possible # of correct items: _____

37. Assessment 2 (name of assessment):   Date of assessment:

Total Score: Scale Score: Passed   or   Failed
Domain Names & scores:

Domain A (name): _____	Domain B: (name): _____	Domain C: (name): _____	Domain D: (name): _____	Domain E: (name): _____	Domain F: (name): _____
Score: (# correct/ possible # of correct items: _____	Score: (# correct/ possible # of correct items: _____	Score: (# correct/ possible # of correct items: _____	Score: (# correct/ possible # of correct items: _____	Score: (# correct/ possible # of correct items: _____	Score: (# correct/ possible # of correct items: _____

38. Assessment 3 (name of assessment):   Date of assessment:

Total Score: Scale Score: Passed   or   Failed

Domain Names & scores:

Domain A (name): _____	Domain B: (name): _____	Domain C: (name): _____	Domain D: (name): _____	Domain E: (name): _____	Domain F: (name): _____
Score: (# correct/ possible # of correct items: _____	Score: (# correct/ possible # of correct items: _____	Score: (# correct/ possible # of correct items: _____	Score: (# correct/ possible # of correct items: _____	Score: (# correct/ possible # of correct items: _____	Score: (# correct/ possible # of correct items: _____

39. Assessment 4 (name of assessment):   Date of assessment:

Total Score: Scale Score: Passed   or   Failed

Domain Names & scores:

Domain A (name): _____	Domain B: (name): _____	Domain C: (name): _____	Domain D: (name): _____	Domain E: (name): _____	Domain F: (name): _____
Score: (# correct/ possible # of correct items: _____	Score: (# correct/ possible # of correct items: _____	Score: (# correct/ possible # of correct items: _____	Score: (# correct/ possible # of correct items: _____	Score: (# correct/ possible # of correct items: _____	Score: (# correct/ possible # of correct items: _____

VI. Referral Information:

40. Name & Title of Referring Person(s).

41. Name & Title of Pre-Referral Team Members. List each person's name, title, and relationship to student.

42. Is this student a minority/culturally diverse student?   Yes   No

If yes, are there any minority/culturally diverse persons a member of the pre-referral team? (including the principal, representative teachers, parent/guardian(s), community members, etc. Yes   No   If yes, list.

VII. Reason(s) for Referral:

43. A review of the available information suggests that this student's educational challenges are most likely due to (check all that apply):

__ Academic   __ Behavioral __ Speech Language   __ Cultural   __ Other:_____

Identify any areas in which the student displays a significant strength (S) or a significant weakness (W). If the skill listed is "not age appropriate" indicate (NAP). Gather annotated work samples that illustrate the student's areas of significant weakness.

Academic Present Levels of Performance (All "W" responses should be flagged)

Reading Readiness:
____   Recognizes letters of the alphabet
____   Demonstrates initial sound fluency (can identify and produce the initial sound in a given word)
____   Demonstrates phonemic segmentation fluency (can identify and produce the initial sounds in a given word)
____   Demonstrates nonsense word fluency (can identify and produce letter sound correspondences and can blend letters together to form "nonsense" words e.g. cag, lew)
____   Recognizes numbers
____   Holds books correctly
____   Uses a pencil correctly
____   Discerns shapes
____   Has some understanding of interpreting illustrations

___ Has some concepts and conventions of print
___ Demonstrates an understanding of left to right (direction of reading/writing process)

Basic Reading: (All "W" responses should be flagged)
___ Recognizes sight words
___ Demonstrates phonemic segmentation fluency (can identify and produce the initial sounds in a given word)
___ Demonstrates oral reading fluency (can read grade level material accurately and fluently)
___ Demonstrates comprehension of text read by self
___ Demonstrates comprehension of text read by others
___ Uses context clues to understand new vocabulary
___ Demonstrates understanding of text read in content areas

Written Language: (All "W" responses should be flagged)
___ Generates logical ideas (prewriting)
___ Focuses on topic (prewriting)
___ Uses prewriting ideas to complete first draft
___ Revises written drafts using descriptive words that expand meaning and provide clarity
___ Focuses on topic during the writing process
___ Writes age/grade appropriate sentences
___ Edits each sentence so all sentences begin with a capital letter
___ Edits each sentence for accurate punctuation
___ Edits each sentence so all proper nouns are capitalized
___ Edits each sentence for correct spelling
___ Uses complete sentences
___ Writes using age/grade appropriate vocabulary
___ Writes 3-5 sentence paragraphs
___ Writes about self-selected topics
___ Uses available technology to assist in writing
___ Prints legibly
___ Uses examples from literature or expository text to write stories and/or complete assignments
___ Answers questions orally when given a topic
___ Answers written multiple-choice questions accurately
___ Answers short answer questions accurately with age/grade level appropriateness
___ Answers essay questions accurately with age/grade level appropriateness
___ Can make oral predictions after reading a story
___ Can make oral predictions after reading an expository text
___ Generates written predictions when asked after reading a story
___ Generates written predictions when asked after reading an expository text
___ Shares writing with others

Math Computation/Calculation: (All "W" responses should be flagged)
___ Counts by rote to appropriate age/grade level
___ Identifies numerical symbols at appropriate age/grade level
___ Demonstrates spatial awareness of symbol placement at appropriate age/grade level
___ Demonstrates an understanding of proper sequence of operations at age/grade level
___ Demonstrates an understanding of addition facts
___ Demonstrates an understanding of subtraction facts
___ Demonstrates an understanding of multiplication facts
___ Demonstrates an understanding of division facts
___ Demonstrates an understanding of place value
___ Demonstrates an understanding of subtraction facts
___ Solves 1-step problems at appropriate age/grade level
___ Solves 2-step problems at appropriate age/grade level

___ Solves multiple step problems at appropriate age/grade level
___ Solves algebraic equations at appropriate age/grade level

Math Reasoning: (All "W" responses should be flagged)
___ Selects correct operations and completes word problems
___ Demonstrates an understanding of addition concepts
___ Demonstrates an understanding of subtraction concepts
___ Demonstrates an understanding of multiplication concepts
___ Demonstrates an understanding of division concepts
___ Correctly identifies money at appropriate age/grade level
___ Demonstrates an understanding of the value of money at appropriate age/grade level
___ Demonstrates an understanding of money and is able to make purchases
___ Demonstrates an understanding of telling time using a digital clock
___ Demonstrates an understanding of telling time using a face clock
___ Demonstrates an understanding of using measurement at appropriate age/grade level
___ Demonstrates an understanding of basic geometry
___ Identifies causal relationships and clearly articulates the connection between cause and effect
___ Analyzes complex problems and provides an organized, well-defined interpretation that includes possible solutions or remedies at appropriate age/grade level
___ Uses examples or counter examples to make a valid argument at appropriate age/grade level
___ Demonstrates effective use of deductive reasoning by making specific judgments from a generalization at appropriate age/grade level
___ Interprets data to make valid conjectures at appropriate age/grade level
___ Formulates a hypothesis and proves or disproves the position at appropriate age/grade level
___ Analyzes problems by identifying relationships, distinguishing relevant from irrelevant information, identifying missing information, sequencing, and prioritizing information, and observing patterns

Behavioral Present Levels of Performance (All "W" responses should be flagged)
Social Behaviors at School:

___ Comes to class prepared
___ Attempts assigned tasks
___ Follows directions
___ Completes class work on time
___ Returns homework on time
___ Works well in groups
___ Works independently
___ Leader
___ Follower
___ Pays attention
___ Easily distracted
___ Participates in class
___ Requests assistance appropriately
___ Takes turns
___ Easily transitions from one activity to another
___ Takes responsibility for actions
___ Works well in structured settings
___ Works well in unstructured settings
___ Happy with self
___ Liked by others

- ___ Plays well with peers
- ___ Socializes appropriately with peers
- ___ Communicates appropriately with peers
- ___ Communicates appropriately with adults
- ___ Requires excessive attention from peers
- ___ Requires excessive attention from adults
- ___ Has very few close friends
- ___ Exhibits uncooperative attitude towards school work
- ___ Exhibits uncooperative attitude towards adults
- ___ Lacks motivation at school
- ___ Has other interests/hobbies other than school
- ___ Lazy and refuses to try
- ___ Does not adjust well to change
- ___ Immature when compared to same age/grade peers
- ___ Trustworthy
- ___ Overly dependent on peers
- ___ Overly dependent on adults
- ___ Overly anxious to please peers
- ___ Overly anxious to please adults
- ___ Manipulative
- ___ Aggressive with peers
- ___ Aggressive with adults
- ___ Fearful of failure
- ___ Bully
- ___ Lies
- ___ Uses offensive language
- ___ Sexually inappropriate
- ___ Cries excessively or at inappropriate times
- ___ Often sad
- ___ Often depressed
- ___ Shy and withdrawn
- ___ Restless
- ___ Sleeps in class
- ___ Daydreams
- ___ Draws/doodles in class
- ___ Loud
- ___ Obnoxious
- ___ Friendly
- ___ Friends with older or younger students
- ___ Has self-control
- ___ Jealous/envious of peers
- ___ Responds appropriately to reprimands/discipline
- ___ Frequent tardies
- ___ Excessive absences
- ___ Frequent in-school suspensions
- ___ Frequent out-of-school suspensions
- ___ Well groomed
- ___ Good personal hygiene

Social Behaviors at Home/Community: (All "W" responses should be flagged)
- ___ Requires excessive attention from parents/guardians
- ___ Requires excessive attention from siblings
- ___ Requires excessive attention from friends
- ___ Accepts discipline/punishment respectfully
- ___ Rebels when disciplined/punished
- ___ Behavior is eliminated when disciplined/punished

___ Behavior improves when disciplined/punished
___ Plays well with siblings
___ Plays well with friends
___ Lacks motivation at home
___ Lazy
___ Interests and/or hobbies
___ Completes assigned chores at home correctly and willingly
___ Overly dependent on siblings
___ Overly dependent on parents/guardians
___ Overly anxious to please siblings
___ Overly anxious to please parents/guardians
___ Manipulative
___ Aggressive with siblings
___ Aggressive with parents/guardians
___ Fearful of failure
___ Lies
___ Uses offensive language
___ Sexually inappropriate
___ Cries excessively or at inappropriate times
___ Often sad
___ Often depressed
___ Shy and withdrawn
___ Daydreams
___ Restless
___ Stays up late
___ Sleeps excessively
___ Obnoxious
___ Wets the bed
___ Friendly
___ Friends older or younger children
___ Has self-control
___ Jealous/envious of siblings
___ Jealous/envious of friends
___ Responds appropriately to reprimands/discipline
___ Takes responsibility for actions
___ Functions well with structure
___ Functions well without structure
___ Feels loved by parents/guardians

Speech Language Present Levels of Performance: (All "W" responses should be flagged)
___ Produces speech sounds (phonology) with age/grade appropriateness (does not exhibit speech sounds characterized by substitutions, omissions, additions, or distortions)
___ Demonstrates appropriate age/grade level comprehension of language
___ Demonstrates appropriate age/grade level use of language
___ Oral expression is age/grade appropriate (speech is understandable)
___ Demonstrates appropriate age/grade level understanding of the structure and

construction of word forms (morphology)

___ Auditory processing is age/grade appropriate (comprehends information presented orally)
___ Uses language in a functional and socially appropriate manner to communicate
___ Communicates without repetitions, hesitations, or prolongations of sounds in words or syllables
___ Communicates with appropriate age/grade level rate, rhythm, quality, pitch, loudness, and resonance
___ Follows verbal directions

___ Attends to speaker
___ Story retelling fluency (can retell a story in an organized and meaningful manner) at appropriate age/grade level
___ Demonstrates an understanding of simple questions and/or requests
___ Speaks with a dialect
___ Use of vocabulary is comparable to peers
___ English as a Second Language (ESL)
___ Culturally & Linguistically Diverse or Minority Student
___ Communicates with peers in an age appropriate manner
___ Communicates with adults in an age appropriate manner

VIII.   Cultural Present Levels of Performance

Part I: Cultural Diversity/Disproportionality Observational Questionnaire
(Part 1 of 2 of the Cultural Present Levels of Performance)

44. Is this student a minority?   Yes   No   If yes, which racial/ethnic group does this student belong? (African American/Black; American-Indian, Asian; Hispanic/Latino, Multi-racial, White, other:

45. Is this student an ESL (English Second Language Learner)?   Yes   No

46. Does this student have difficulty learning language at a normal rate? Yes   No
    If yes, explain:

47. Does this student have deficits in vocabulary?   Yes   No

48. Does this student have difficulties communicating at school?   Yes   No If yes, explain.

49. Does this student have difficulty communicating at home?   Yes   No
        If yes, explain:

50. Does this student have difficulty interacting with peers from a similar background?
    Yes   No   If yes, explain:

51. Has this problem been observed in the student's first and second language?
    Yes   No
    If yes, explain how well the student performed in his/her first language.

52. Does this student have any auditory processing problems (e.g. poor memory, poor comprehension, etc.) Yes   No   If yes, explain:

53. Does this student have adequate English proficiency, but slow academic achievement?
Yes   No   If yes, explain:

54. Does this student rely heavily on gestures, pictures, and/or symbols rather than speech
to communicate? Yes   No   If yes, explain:

55. Does this student respond slowly to questions as compared to same age/grade
peers/siblings? Yes   No   If yes, explain:

56. Is this student typically disorganized and/or confused in the school setting? Yes   No
If yes, explain:

57. Does this student have difficulty paying attention/staying on task in school? Yes   No
If yes, explain:

58. Does this student have a need for frequent repetition and/or prompts during instruction?
Yes No
If yes, explain:

59. Does this student learn at a normal rate when provided with adequate instruction?
Yes   No   If no, explain:

60. Does this student require a more structured program of instruction than same age/grade
level peers? Yes   No   If yes, explain:

61. Does this student have difficulty using appropriate grammar and sentence structure?
Yes   No
If yes, explain:

62. Does this student have difficulty using specific vocabulary and instead uses
words/phrases such as "stuff", "things", "you know"? Yes   No
If yes, explain:

63. Does this student have an inappropriate social use of language (e.g. interrupts others when speaking, digresses from topic, insensitive/unaware of the communication goals of conversational partners, cannot/does not take turns in conversation, etc.)?
        Yes   No
        If yes, explain:

64. Does this student exhibit poor communication sequencing skills (e.g. communication is disorganized, incoherent, leaves listener confused, etc.)?   Yes   No
If yes, explain:

65. Is this student's overall ability to communicate substantially lower than his/her same age/grade peers? Yes No   If yes, explain:

66. Does the referring teacher(s) assume that the problem is the result of the child having a disability or that it results from being an ESL student?   Yes   No   If yes, explain:

67. Does the referring teacher(s) have sufficient knowledge of the second language acquisition process?   Yes   No   If no, explain supports needed:

68. Does the referring teacher(s) believe in cultural assimilation? (The minority group is to assimilate into the belief systems and practices of the larger group).   Yes   No
    Explain.

69. Does the referring teacher(s) believe in the co-existence of cultures which are valued equally?   Yes   No

70. Does the referring teacher(s) have a personal interest in learning more about the culture of the student being referred?   Yes   No

71. Has the team determined which delays are the result of the student's cultural transition into the United States, school, and/or community? Yes   No

        If yes, explain:

72. Has the team made home visits to conduct ethnographic interviews to learn about the student's home life and that of his parents?   Yes   No
        If yes, provide insights that may be helpful in providing appropriate educational assistance to the student.

73. Has the referring teacher(s) maintained a two-way dialogue around evidenced-based strategies that both teachers and family members can use to assist the student?
        Yes   No   If yes, explain:

74. Has the referring teacher(s) documented when the problem behaviors are occurring along with their frequency and intensity compared to same age/grade level peers?
        Yes   No   If yes, explain:

75. Has the referring teacher(s) modified his/her instruction and/or classroom to meet the needs of culturally and linguistically diverse students?   Yes   No

        If yes, explain:

76. Has the referring teacher(s) assigned a peer buddy to the student (preferably one with a similar language and/or cultural background) for selected activities?   Yes   No
        Explain:

77. Has the referring teacher(s) identified any school or community role models for the student with whom they could bond and communicate with?   Yes   No
        If no, explain:

78. Do the parents/guardians report that their child has difficulty learning the language spoken in the home at a normal rate? Yes   No   If yes, explain:

79. Do the parents/guardians assume that the problem is the result of the child having a disability or that the problem is a result of their child speaking another language?
        Yes   No   Explain:

80. Does this student have a family history of special education and/or learning difficulties?
        Yes   No
        If yes, indicate who: ___ mother ___ father ___ sister ___ brother ___ other: ___

What area(s) of special education and/or learning disability are they identified with?

81. Have the parents/guardians stated that this child had slower development than his/her other siblings?
Yes   No   If yes, explain:

82. Have the parents/guardians stated this child is typically disorganized and/or confused in the home environment? Yes   No   If yes, explain:

83. Have the parents/guardians stated that this child has difficulty paying attention/staying on task at home? Yes   No   If yes, explain:

84. Are the parents or guardians of this student actively involved in their child's schooling?
Yes   No

85. Did the parents/guardians have a positive personal experience with school?

Yes   No

86. Do the parents/guardians think education is important for their child's overall success in life?   Yes   No   Explain.

87. Do the parents/guardians feel that school personnel respect their cultural beliefs?
Yes   No
If no, explain:

88. Have parents/guardians been actively participating in the pre-referral team meetings and have they been treated as respected and knowledgeable members of the team with unique insights and contributions? Yes   No   If no, explain:

89. Are standardized tests being given in the student's first language? Yes   No
If no, explain:

90. Would a translation of the test in the student's first language be sufficient to make it appropriate for the content to be assessed?   Yes   No   Explain:

91. Have standardized tests been examined for linguistic and cultural bias relative to the student's background?   Yes   No   Don't know

92. Have the standardized tests administered been normed on the race/ethnicity group of the referred student to determine if it is appropriate?   Yes   No   Don't know

93. Have any accommodations or modifications been provided on standardized tests taken by this student? Yes   No   If yes, explain:

94. Have error analysis been conducted on class work, informal, and/or formal assessments?   Yes   No   If yes, explain.

IX. Specific Learning Disability Exclusionary Factors

95. Check all factors that apply to the student. Information can be obtained from multiple sources such as student records, interviews with parents/guardians, teachers, etc.

Instruction:
- ❑ Lack of appropriate instruction in reading which includes the 5 essential components of reading (phonemic awareness, phonics, fluency, vocabulary, & comprehension)
- ❑ Lack of appropriate instruction in math
- ❑ Lack of appropriate instruction in writing
- ❑ Visual, hearing, or motor disability

Environmental:
- ❑ Lack of adequate communication (verbal, written, etc.)
- ❑ Lack of opportunity/limited experiences
- ❑ Lack of encouragement
- ❑ Lack of inspiration
- ❑ Lack of motivation
- ❑ Home responsibilities conflict with learning opportunities
- ❑ Excessive absences in school

Economic Disadvantage:
- ❑ Free/reduced lunch
- ❑ Homeless or residence is in a depressed economic area
- ❑ Family income falls within the lowest economic levels

Cultural:
- ❑ Limited English proficiency
- ❑ Limited involvement with or knowledge of activities or organizations of the majority-based culture
- ❑ Limited experience with the majority-based culture
- ❑ Geographic remoteness
- ❑ Home standards in conflict with majority-based cultural standards

Atypical Educational History:
- ❑ Irregular school attendance
- ❑ Attendance at multiple schools

Other:
- ❑ Intellectual Disabilities
- ❑ Emotional Disturbances

❑ Visual, hearing, or motor disability

Are the above checked items compelling enough to indicate this student's educational performance is primarily due to environmental, cultural, or economic disadvantage? For students with Limited English Proficiency, take into consideration if the student speaks another language other than English, how long has the student spoken English, is there another language spoken in the student's home, is the student receiving Limited English Proficiency services? If there is enough compelling evidence to support the student's educational performance concerns are primarily due to environmental, cultural, or economic disadvantage, this excludes this student from being referred for special education services. However, this student may benefit from receiving other research-based academic, behavioral, speech-language and/or other appropriate services to help remediate their performance.

X. Part II: Educator Self-Evaluation Cultural Considerations Intervention Rating Scale
(Part 2 of 2 of the Cultural Present Levels of Performance)

Directions: Rate your level of application, use, consistency, and expertise in implementing the following for culturally and linguistic diverse and/or struggling students.
(0 = Never; 1 = Very Rarely; 2 = Rarely; 3 = Occasionally; 4 = Very Frequently; 5 = Frequently)
(All responses of 0, 1, 2, & 3 should be flagged). Use the results from this section to determine if the teacher/practitioner needs additional support in order to best meet the needs of the student(s) he/she serves.

96. Motivate student learning   0   1   2   3   4   5

97. Use of activating/hook activities to gain student attention
    0   1   2   3   4   5

98. Instructional accommodations (changes in "how" instruction, information, assessments, etc. are provided)   0   1   2   3   4   5

99. Instructional modification (significant changes in "what" the student is expected to learn and/or demonstrate)   0   1   2   3   4   5

100. Changes in the "process" in which the student accesses material
    0   1   2   3   4   5

101. Changes in the "product" in which student learning is evidenced
    0   1   2   3   4   5

102. Environment (general education, inclusion, resource, self-contained) in which content is taught   0   1   2   3   4   5

103. Instructional grouping   0   1   2   3   4   5

104. Differentiating instruction   0   1   2   3   4   5

105. Differentiating instruction based on student's multiple intelligence areas of strength
    0   1   2   3   4   5

106. Differentiating of performance assessments 0   1   2   3   4   5

107. Adjusting rate of instruction   0   1   2   3   4   5

108. Allowing additional time for student's processing of information
    0   1   2   3   4   5

109. Speaking clearly and audibly   0   1   2   3   4   5
110. Rephrasing and restating information   0   1   2   3   4   5

111. Providing instruction based on student's readiness/skill level
    0   1   2   3   4   5

112. Use of instructional modifications   0   1   2   3   4   5

113. Providing safe environments for all student responses
    0   1   2   3   4   5

114. Providing instruction considering student's interest
    0   1   2   3   4   5

115. Providing instruction based on student's learning profile
    0   1   2   3   4   5

116. Preview new material   0   1   2   3   4   5

117. Review previous material   0   1   2   3   4   5

118. Frequent checks for comprehension   0   1   2   3   4   5

119. Progress monitoring of student learning   0   1   2   3   4   5

120. Adjusting instruction based on student data   0   1   2   3   4   5

121. Use of alternative assessments to assess student's understanding
    0   1   2   3   4   5

122. Focus on teaching meaning rather than covering content
    0   1   2   3   4   5

123. Allowing extended "wait time" to answer questions
    0   1   2   3   4   5

124. Providing extra attention for students who need it
    0   1   2   3   4   5

125. Encourage/respect student's use and development of their primary language
    0   1   2   3   4   5

126. Encourage students to include their own cultural experiences and background into learning experiences
    0   1   2   3   4   5

127. Include multicultural activities and materials into instruction on a regular basis
    0   1   2   3   4   5

128. Encourage and include parents/community members from different cultural backgrounds to participate in teaching/learning experiences of my students

0   1   2   3   4   5

***Items marked 3 and below should be <u>considered</u> for implementation of research-based instructional strategies. Instructional strategies should be implemented consistently with fidelity over a sufficient amount of time. Data on student performance should be collected and progress monitored so appropriate instructional decisions can be made.

XI. Social History & Family Data:

Student's Name

Student's Address:

     City:

     State/Province:

     Zip/Postal Code:

Parent's Marital Status: married   separated   divorced   deceased (mother, father, both)

Parent/Guardian #1 (mother, father, grandmother, aunt, other: ____):

Age: ___

Parent/Guardian's Address (if different from student's):

City:

     State/Province:

     Zip/Postal Code:

Home Number:

Parent/Guardian's Place of Employment:

Work Number:

Cell/Alternative Number:

Email Address #1:   Email Address #2:   Email Address #3:

Education Level of Parent/Guardian #1: drop-out   high school   college graduate

Is there any known use of drug use/abuse? Yes No   If yes, explain:

Relationship and type of interaction with non-custodial parent: excellent   good   fair   poor

Parent/Guardian #1 (mother, father, grandmother, aunt, other: ____):

Age: ___

Parent/Guardian's Address (if different from student's):

City:

     State/Province:

     Zip/Postal Code:

Home Number:

Parent/Guardian's Place of Employment:

Work Number:

Cell/Alternative Number:

Email Address #1:   Email Address #2:   Email Address #3:

Education Level of Parent/Guardian #2: drop-out high school   college graduate

Is there any known use of drug use/abuse? Yes No   If yes, explain: _____

Previous Schools Attended:

     Most recent school attended (other than present school) _____

     Name(s) of School: Year(s) Attended:

     Number of Schools Attended Within System _____   Outside System _____

129.   List any subjects that are especially difficult for your child.

130.   Describe any serious problems your child has experienced at school.

131.   Describe any serious problems your child has experienced at home.

132.   Describe your child's study habits at home.

133.   Who is the primary person who helps your child with his/her homework?

134.   How much time is spent on homework each night?

135.   What time does your child wake up for school?

136.   What time does your child go to bed on school nights?

137.   How many people live in the home with your child?

138.   How would you define your child's home neighborhood as it relates to safety?
        Dangerous   Unsafe   Somewhat-Safe   Safe   Very-Safe

139.   How would you define your child's home environment as it relates to safety, security, and
        living conditions?
        Dangerous   Unsafe   Somewhat-Safe   Safe   Very-Safe

140.   Agencies or specialists that have worked with this student or family and contacts:

Mental Health: ___   Contact Person: ___   Address: ___   Date Seen: ___

Physician: _____   Contact Person: ___   Address: ___   Date Seen: ___

Social Worker _____   Contact Person: ___   Address: ___   Date Seen: ___

Babies Can't Wait: _____   Contact Person: ___   Address: ___   Date Seen: ___

Other _____   Contact Person: ___   Address: ___   Date Seen: ___

Other _____   Contact Person: ___   Address: ___   Date Seen: ___

141.   Are there any members of the immediate family incarcerated?   Yes   No   If yes, list:

Mother   Years Incarcerated ___

Father   Years Incarcerated ___

Brother Years Incarcerated ___

Sister   Years Incarcerated ___

Other: Years Incarcerated ___

142.   Does the student communicate with the incarcerated family member?   Yes   No

If yes, how does the student react after communicating with the family member?   Yes   No

If yes, how does the student react?

XII. Student's Birth & Developmental History:

Full Term Pregnancy: Yes   No   If no, how many weeks of gestation at birth?

Did the mother smoke, drink, or use illegal drugs during the pregnancy? Yes   No
        If yes, list the substances used.

Did the mother experience clinical depression before, during, or after the pregnancy? Yes No
        If yes, explain.

Is there a history of mental illness on the mother's or father's side of the family? Yes   No If yes, explain.

List any illnesses, accidents, or traumatic events that occurred during pregnancy.

Birth Weight: _____   Length of Labor: _____
Type of Delivery: Normal   Breech   Cesarean
Was there any evidence of injury at birth: Yes   No   If yes, explain.

Were any of the following experienced before your child's second birthday?
___Feeding problems   ___Convulsions___High fever
___Fainting   ___Serious accidents   ___Head injuries   ___Other:
Explain all items checked above:

Does/did your child have a history of ear infections?   Yes   No

Does your child exhibit any unusual behaviors when playing alone, with peers, and/or with adults? Yes   No   If yes, explain.

Did your child meet developmental milestones at age appropriate times (ex. Crawling, rolling over, walking, speaking (saying first word; making requests, responding accurately to requests), sitting up, toilet trained, tied shoes, dressing self, etc.) Yes   No   If no, explain areas that were delayed.

Has your child's physician ever expressed concerns over any issues such as your baby's weight, activity level, developmental rates, responses, growth pattern, etc.? Yes   No
If yes, explain.

XIII.Child's Current Physical, Mental/Emotional Health:

Has your child ever been diagnosed with any significant illnesses or disorders, excluding typical childhood or seasonal illnesses such as colds, strep, flu, etc.? Yes   No   If yes, explain.

Does your child have allergies? Yes   No   If yes, what kind of allergies does he/she have and is he/she taking medications? Please list medications & dosage.

Has your child ever seen a psychologist or psychiatrist? Yes   No   If yes, how long and why? _____ Were any medications prescribed? If so, what and what was the dosage?

Is your child currently seeing a psychologist or psychiatrists? Yes   No   If yes, why?

Is your child currently taking any prescribed medications to assist with their mental or emotional health? Yes   No   If yes, what kind and what is the dosage?

If your child is NOT currently seeing a psychologist or psychiatrists, do you think it would be beneficial to your child? Yes   No   Explain why or why not.

Do you feel your child is in good physical and/or mental/emotional health? Yes   No, If no, explain.

Additional information and/or concerns:

XIV. **Summary of Findings and Analysis of Comprehensive At-Risk Questionnaire**

Describe areas of strength, weakness, and recommendations. Then complete ABC's of RTI Data Collection and Documentation Form.

RTI & Behavior: Tier 3 (Tertiary Prevention)

Tier 3, tertiary preventions deal with the smallest percentage (1% - 7%) of students in the behavioral pyramid who require intensive and individualized behavioral supports to meet their needs. Within the RTI multi-tiered service delivery model, Tier 2 and beyond (Tier 3) research-based interventions provide local school systems with the first line of defense for reducing the number of students with challenging behaviors. The use of functional behavior assessments (FBA) strategies and behavior intervention plans (BIP) assist in the development of individualized behavior supports needed to determine if a student should be referred on for special education determination.

Providing timely and evidence-based behavior and instructional strategies to at-risk students can make the difference between at-risk students successfully returning to the general education classroom or them being referred on for special education evaluation (Compton, Fuchs, & Fuchs, 2006). It is important to note that Tier 2 and beyond (Tier 3) intervention is for students for whom Tier 1 behavioral instruction is insufficient, who are falling behind on benchmark skills, and who require additional instruction to achieve grade-level academic or behavioral expectations. Tier 2 and beyond interventions consists of general education instruction *plus* specialized intervention (Tier 1 + Tier 2 + Tier 3) that take into consideration results from previous intervention and:

Size of instructional group. Tier 2 and beyond (Tier 3) instruction is provided in small groups (two to four students).

Mastery requirements of behavior and content. Cut scores identified on screening measures and continued growth as demonstrated by routine progress monitoring are indicators of behavioral and/or content mastery.

Frequency of progress monitoring. Even though recommendations vary, weekly progress monitoring to three times per week is standard. It is important to progress monitor with the frequency recommended in research-based practices. However, it is also important to follow state and district level established criteria for progress monitoring at each tier.

Duration of the intervention. Tier 2 and beyond (Tier 3) interventions typically last between 9 to 12 weeks and can be repeated as needed (see specific state/district level criteria).

Frequency with which the intervention is delivered. Tier 2 and beyond (Tier 3) provides for three to four intervention sessions per week, each lasting between 30 to 60 minutes (see specific state/district level criteria).

Instructor qualifications. Instruction is conducted by trained and supervised personnel (not the classroom teacher) in the Tier 3 model. This may differ in other models. (see specific state/district level criteria).

In Tiers 1, 2, and 3, it is imperative to provide research-based interventions specific to a student's identified academic and behavioral needs. Even though students have unique needs, there is a body of research that suggests that when teachers implement a core set of teaching principles, it is likely that all their students will be successful. According to Martens and Meller (1990), strategies that tend to promote success for all students are:

1. Ensure that students are being taught at the optimal instructional level, one that challenges the student, but provides enough success to keep them invested and confident in learning.
2. Provide "scaffolding" support (individual instructional modifications) to students as necessary to help them to learn a new task or keep up with more advanced learners. Examples of scaffolding strategies include reducing the number of problems assigned to a student, permitting the student to use technological aids (e.g., word processing software which predicts student word selection to reduce keyboarding), and using cooperative learning groups that pool their knowledge to complete assignments.
3. Model and demonstrate explicit strategies to students for learning academic material or completing assignments. Have them use these strategies under supervision until you are sure that students understand and can correctly use them.
4. Make sure that students who are mastering new academic skills have frequent opportunities to practice these skills with immediate corrective feedback.
5. Provide lots of opportunities for students to drill, practice, and review previously learned skills or material to help them to retain this information.

Each of these strategies can be extended to include social skills and expected behaviors as well.

Remember, Tier 3, tertiary interventions are for students with chronic behavior problems who did not respond to Tier 1 or Tier 2 interventions. At Tier 3, schools need to conduct a comprehensive in-depth analysis of all student data gathered at Tier 1 and Tier 2. Individualized supports are to be provided at Tier 3. Tier 3 is when a brief or in-depth Functional Behavior Assessment (FBA) should be conducted (as determined by the team) incorporated with evidenced-based interventions that should be implemented with fidelity within the Behavior Intervention Plan (BIP). It is essential at Tier 3 that an array of assessment information be gathered to aid in the problem solving process to determine the appropriate supports. Tier 3 supports require significantly more amounts of staff time and expertise. However, because these students' behavioral challenges have shown at this point to be persistent and intense, the need for additional time to remediate their behavior problems is warranted. Progress monitoring in Tier 3 is as essential to the problem solving process as it was in Tier 1 and Tier 2. Monitoring responsiveness to intervention along with implementation fidelity is crucial in effective team decision making.

Following is a table of step-by-step instructions for implementing RTI & Behavior in Tier 3. This table is to be used as a guide for implementation along with the sample data collection forms.

Steps in the RTI & Behavior Implementation Process
Tier 3

Tier 3	Tier 3 is provided to all at-risk students who did not respond to Tier 2 research-based academic and/or behavioral interventions. Students in need of Tier 3 interventions are determined by examining data and student responsiveness when a student has received ex. 9 to 12 weeks of interventions at Tier 2 and are still not on trajectory to benchmark at their academic grade level and/or behavioral expectations.
Focus of Tier 3	The focus of Tier 3 requires intensive, individualized high-quality instruction matched to student need. Tier 3 occurs in addition to Tier 1 and Tier 2. Tier 3 may occur within the general education classroom initially, but must occur within a smaller group than in Tier 2 interventions. If a student has not progressed in Tier 2 after e.g. 9 to 12 weeks of targeted instruction focused on the student's area(s) of identified need, Tier 3 recommends a minimum of 150 minutes of intensive individualized intervention focused on the student's area(s) of identified need(s) and is recommended across a minimum of 4 sessions. In the case of students with needs in reading and math, a minimum of 180 minutes of intervention is mandated. Behavior deficits are to be addressed in conjunction with academic deficits. In either case, the duration of each session should be appropriate to the age and development of the child. *(Note: The law speaks to the minimum required and is not necessarily the standard for best practice, or meeting the targeted needs of each student).* *After a student has received between e.g. between 9 to 12 weeks in Tier 1 PLUS, 9 to 12 weeks in Tier 2 PLUS 9 to 12 weeks in Tier 3, and still is not progressing or is not on trajectory to be on benchmark by the end of the year, the intervention team shall refer the student for initial evaluation for special education services. At this point the intervention team should have sufficient information to rule out a number of critical factors that can interfere with the student's learning and the team will have a good idea of the types of diagnostic assessment that still may be needed.*
Examples of data to be examined	Discipline/office referrals, attendance, tardies, suspensions, grades, test scores (formal & informal), juvenile justice records, family crisis (homelessness, divorce, death, unemployment, abuse, neglect, etc. – use professional judgment)
What happens at Tier 3	• Tier 1 + Tier 2 + Tier 3

*Follow the same steps as in Tier 2. The difference between Tier 2 and Tier 3 is the intensity of the interventions and the minutes of intervention.

- Continue teaching core curriculum with fidelity
- Secondary preventions/interventions are provided to at-risk students who did not respond to Tier 2 interventions using Standard Protocol and/or Problem Solving
- Supplemental social behavioral support is added to reduce the current number and intensity of problem behavior
- Addresses problems that are of a chronic nature or a severe magnitude
- Interventions are more individualized than Tier 2
- Differentiation is different and more individualized than Tier 2
- Intensive individualized interventions are developed for at-risk students
- Use research-based, scientifically validated interventions and continue delivering core curriculum with fidelity
- Develop a system for increasing structure and predictability
- Develop a system for increasing contingent adult feedback
- Develop a system for linking academic and behavioral performance
- Develop a system for increasing home/school communication
- Progress monitoring at-risk students in deficit areas (e.g. at least bi-weekly for e.g. 9 to 12 weeks – refer to state/district criteria)
- Collect and use data for instructional and behavioral decision-making
- Teams use instructional and behavioral assessments to identify students not mastering behavioral skills at the same rate as peers

After a student has received between e.g. between 9 to 12 weeks in Tier 1 PLUS, 9 to 12 weeks in Tier 2 PLUS 9 to 12 weeks in Tier 3, and still is not progressing or is not on trajectory to be on benchmark by the end of the year, the intervention team shall refer the student for initial evaluation for special education services. At this point the intervention team should have sufficient information to rule out a number of critical factors that can interfere with the student's learning and the team will have a good idea of the types of diagnostic assessment that may still be needed.

Examples of Tier 3 Interventions	<ul><li>Tier 1 + Tier 2 + Tier 3</li><li>Functional Behavior Assessment and team based comprehensive assessments</li><li>Individualized intervention based on FBA data focusing on:<ol><li>Prevention of problem contexts</li><li>Instruction on functionally equivalent skills</li><li>Instruction on desired performance skills</li><li>Strategies for placing problem behaviors on extinction</li><li>Strategies for enhancing contingency reward of desired behavior</li><li>Collection and use of FBA data for BIP development</li></ol></li><li>Behavior Intervention Plans</li><li>Individualized Counseling/Therapy</li><li>Frequent/daily mentoring</li><li>Wrap-around services</li></ul>
Steps to Implementing Tier 3	
Step 1	Identify students needing intensive individualized interventions/tier 3 (e.g. those performing at or below the lowest 20%; or students performing at or below the 25th percentile on a screening measure; or students performing at or below a pre-determined cut score) from those meeting benchmark/Tier 2 etc.
Step 2	Determine and document how to best meet Tier 3 students' specific academic and/or behavioral needs with grade level or content level team members using the standard protocol and/or problem solving treatment model. Data source examples: attendance records, discipline records (e.g. suspension, expulsion, office referrals, non-compliance data, etc.), semester grades, results of curriculum based measurements (CBM), results of formal and/or informal assessments, formative assessments and/or summative assessments, etc.
Step 3	Determine person(s) responsible for implementing instruction/intervention, their title, type of intervention, length of intervention, and location of services.

Step 4	Provide research-based, scientifically validated targeted interventions matched to student's need. Implement with fidelity. Remember intervention must occur for a minimum of 9 to 12 weeks with weekly progress monitoring (see district/state criteria).

Step 5	1. Chart data and begin with the initial scores received on the universal screening and include data from Tier 2 & Tier 3 interventions.
	2. Chart goal line and chart progress. Remember you need a minimum of 3 to 5 data points on goal line to judge if progress is sufficient and further decision making can be determined.
	3. Chart end of the year benchmark/goal.
	4. Determine if intervention is successful based on a problem solving method, established benchmarks, learning rate and level of performance, and document team decision to continue, modify, or change intervention. Possible questions to consider:
	    a. Was the core curriculum and intervention delivered with fidelity?
	    b. Did the intervention match the student's specific area of need?
	    c. Was the teacher/ interventionist trained to deliver the intervention?
	    d. Did the student attend all scheduled sessions of the intervention?
	    e. Did the student receive differentiated needs-based instruction?
	    f. Is the student making progress?
	    g. Is the student making progress, but not yet on target to meet benchmark?
	    h. Does the student's performance differ greatly from his/her age/grade level peers?
	    i. Is the student not making sufficient progress to be on trajectory toward meeting benchmark(s)?
	    j. What strategies/interventions are needed to help this student make progress?

Step 6	• Identify students who were successful in Tier 3 and will return to Tier 2 • Identify students who are making adequate progress, but are not yet meeting benchmark(s) and will remain in Tier 3 (Student Support Team) • Identify students that will be referred for initial evaluation for special education services • Complete the Tier 3 Tertiary Prevention Data Collection &

	Intervention Documentation Form • Review and complete as needed all other relevant Tier 3 recommended forms • Complete any other district or state level required documents for Tier 3

ABC's of Response to Intervention (RTI)
Data Collection & Intervention Documentation Forms

Student's Name: _____ Grade: _____
Date of Birth: _____ Student ID#: _____
School & District: _____ Homeroom Teacher: _____ Content: _____

	Tier 3 – Tertiary Prevention (Sustained, Intensive, Individualized Interventions)
Who:	Ex. General education teacher, specialized teacher, or special education teacher as determined by state and district criteria Specify:
What:	Ex. Core Curriculum and/or individualized instruction as determined by state and district criteria Specify:
Where:	Ex. General Education Classroom or Special Education Classroom as determined by state and district criteria Specify:
How:	Ex. Two 30 minute sessions per day of sustained, intensive, individualized instruction/interventions provided in a one-on-one format and no more than a one-to-three format PLUS Tier 1 & Tier 2 core instruction for 90 minutes per day in targeted area Specify:
Time:	Ex. Minimum of 9 to 12 weeks or as determined by state and district criteria Specify:
Assessment:	Ex. Progress monitoring occurs at least bi-weekly for a minimum of 9 to 12 weeks or as determined by state and/or district criteria Specify:
Description of the Problem:	
Student's Current Performance Level:	
Tier 3 Instruction/ Intervention Goal:	
Instruction/ Intervention Options:	• Option 1: • Option 2:

	• Option 3:
Instruction/ Intervention Implemented & Dates, How, Frequency, and Duration of Implementation (ex. 9 to 12 weeks; two 30 minute sessions per day of intensive individualized instruction/ intervention in a 1:1 no more than 1:3 format PLUS 90 minutes of core instruction in targeted area of need:	• Name & brief description of selected instruction/intervention Option: • Implementation date & ending date: • How was the instruction/intervention implemented: • Duration & frequency of intervention/instruction (ex. number of weeks, number of days per week, number of minutes per day):
Person(s) Responsible for Implementing Instruction/ Intervention, Title, Name of Intervention, Length of Intervention, and Location of Services, and Follow-Up Date(s):	• Name: • Title: • Location: • Name of Intervention: • Length of Intervention: • Location of Service: • Follow-Up Date(s):
Fidelity & Validity Statement:	• I certify that the above referenced Tier 3 intervention/instruction was implemented consistently and reliably as described. _____ Signature, Title, & Date of Person(s) Responsible for Implementing Tier 3 Instruction/Intervention
Progress Monitoring Data & Results: (see progress monitoring graphs)	• Performance Level: • Rate of Growth: • Evaluation Criteria:
Team Decision & Explanation for Tier 3:	❑ Tier 3 instruction/intervention successful – exit Tier 3 and return to Tier 2 instruction/intervention ❑ Problem has not been resolved but progress is being made –

	continue with Tier 3 instruction/intervention provided by the Student Support Team
	❑ Problem not resolved MODIFY Tier 3 instruction/intervention
	❑ Problem not resolved CHANGE Tier 3 instruction/intervention to:
	_____
	❑ Problem not resolved performance level and/or rate of growth remain below acceptable levels – follow district and state guidelines and recommend a comprehensive evaluation take place to determine if the student is eligible for special education services
	❑ Brief Explanation of Team Decision:

ABC's of RTI and Behavior
Classroom Variable Efficacy Checklist

This checklist can be used as an informal assessment to evaluate the efficacy of instruction and instructional environments by examining multiple variables and their impact on student academic and behavioral success.

Teacher: _____ Date: _____ Grade: _____

Content Area Taught: _____

Circle Setting: General   Collaborative   Resource   Self-Contained

Other: _____

Physical Setting:	Yes	No
1. Clean and well-organized		
2. Desk size and classroom setup appropriate for all students		
3. Lighting appropriate		
4. Temperature settings adequate		
5. Noise level acceptable		
6. Conducive to learning		
7. Space is adequate for the number and size of the students in the classroom		
8. Visually attractive and not "overly" stimulating		
9. Student seating arrangements are determined based on student academic and/or behavioral need		
10. Student, teacher, academic, behavioral, and/or instructional factors are considered in proximity control		
Instructional Proficiency:	Yes	No
11. Academic expectations are clearly defined		
12. Students demonstrate an understanding of what they are to know, understand, and be able to do		
13. Performance criteria are explicit and are clearly defined		
14. Differentiation instruction is provided for students identified with need		
15. Assessment is effectively matched to instruction		
16. Assessment results drive instruction (formative & summative data)		
17. Instructional grouping is appropriate for learning		
18. Content and performance standards are clearly defined		
19. Students are actively engaged in instruction		
20. Instruction is provided in various modalities		
Behavior Management Proficiency:	Yes	No
21. Assistance is provided with equity and in a timely manner		
22. Behavioral expectations are communicated using positive behavioral language		
23. Students demonstrate an understanding of the rules and consequences of their behavior		
24. Students are motivated to learn		
25. Behavior management plan is age/grade appropriate for students		
26. Behavior management plan is effective		
27. Safe learning environment		
28. Behavior Intervention Plans are effective		
29. Behavior Intervention Plans are based on the results of Functional Behavioral Assessments		
30. Modeling of appropriate social skills are demonstrated and reinforced		

Discuss the environmental, instructional, and behavioral proficiencies and deficiencies and their effectiveness or lack of effectiveness.

Physical Setting Areas of Proficiency:	Effective or Ineffective Why?	Areas of Deficiency:	Effective or Ineffective Why?
1.	1.	1.	1.
2.	2.	2.	2.
3.	3.	3.	3.
4.	4.	4.	4.
5.	5.	5.	5.
Instructional Proficiency Areas of Proficiency:	Effective or Ineffective Why?	Areas of Deficiency:	Effective or Ineffective Why?
1.	1.	1.	1.
2.	2.	2.	2.
3.	3.	3.	3.
4.	4.	4.	4.
5.	5.	5.	5.
Behavior Management Proficiency Areas of Proficiency:	Effective or Ineffective Why?	Areas of Deficiency:	Effective or Ineffective Why?
1.	1.	1.	1.
2.	2.	2.	2.
3.	3.	3.	3.
4.	4.	4.	4.
5.	5.	5.	5.

Comments:

ABC's of RTI & Behavior
Functional Behavioral Assessment & Behavior Intervention Plans Checklist

This form can be used by Intervention Teams and/or IEP Teams to guide and assess the writing, development, and implementation of functional behavioral assessments and behavioral intervention plans.

Student: _____ Date: _____

Grade: _____ Referring Teacher: _____

Team Members (identify team leader, grades, & subjects taught):

_____   _____

_____   _____

Problem Behavior(s):

_____

_____

_____

Yes	No	
		1. Student's problem behaviors are clearly defined in observable & measurable terms.
		2. Replacement behaviors that serve the same function for the student are identified.
		3. Conditions in which the replacement behaviors for the student should occur are listed.
		4. At least 3 indirect measures (e.g. checklists, rating scales, interviews, questionnaires, etc.) from multiple sources (e.g. teachers, parents, students, etc.) are provided that show multiple occurrences or non-occurrences of the problem behavior in the context in which it occurs.
		5. At least 2 direct measures (e.g. scatterplots, ABC charts, direct observations, manipulation of variables, etc.) from multiple sources (e.g. teachers, parents, students, etc.) are provided that show multiple occurrences or non-occurrences of the problem behavior in the context in which it occurs.
		6. Findings from the indirect and direct measures support the same identified function of the problem behavior with confidence and reliability.
		7. Alternative acceptable behaviors (temporary) have been clearly defined (observable & measurable) for each tier.
		8. Desired behaviors (terminal) are clearly defined (observable & measurable).
		9. The function (reason) for the behavior is identified in the functional behavioral assessment.
		10. A hypotheses statement is written in a contingency format so a behavior intervention plan can be developed. e.g. *Under X conditions, the student will do Y, in order to attain Z.*
		11. The behavior intervention plan is written in the A-B-C (antecedent-behavior-consequence) format.
		12. The behavior intervention plan is developed based on the identified function of the problem behavior in the functional behavioral assessment.
		13. The behavior intervention plan addresses both the academic and behavioral needs of the student.
		14. The behavior intervention plan addresses all the social and environmental contexts in which the problem behavior occurs.
		15. The functional behavioral assessment and behavior intervention plan include progress monitoring with sufficient data to support the behavior intervention plans effectiveness.
		15. The functional behavioral assessment and behavior intervention plan are implemented effectively.

ABC's of RTI and Behavior
Student Daily Schedule & Behavioral Ratings
(To be used as FBA Documentation)

This form can be used as a source to determine the function (reason) for a student's problem behavior. Information should be completed by the teacher or person serving the student during the scheduled time. This information is to be used in conjunction with other data to determine the function of behavior and to develop and implement the behavior intervention plan. Place an "X" in each column to rate the intensity, times, and classes in which the student exhibits the problem behaviors.

Student: _____ Date: _____
Grade: _____ Age: _____ Respondent's Name: _____
Title/Content Taught: _____

Subject Teacher	Before School	1st Period	Transition	2nd Period	Transition	3rd Period	Transition	4th Period	Lunch	5th Period	Transition	6th Period	After School
5 Extremely Intense													
4													
3													
2													
1 Not Intense													

Do you think the student's problem behavior is "to avoid something" or "to get something". Explain.

Student Daily Schedule & Behavioral Ratings **PARENT VERSION**
(To be used as FBA Documentation)

This form can be used as a source to determine the function (reason) for a student's problem behavior. Information should be completed by a parent/guardian. Describe intense problem behaviors that occur at home and rate its level of intensity from 1 (not intense) to 5 (extremely intense). This information is to be used in conjunction with other data to determine the function of behavior and to develop and implement the behavior intervention plan. Place an "X" in each column to rate the intensity, times, and specifics related to the occurrence of when your child exhibits the problem behaviors.

Student: _____ Date: _____

Grade: _____ Age: _____ Parent/Guardian's Name: _____

Problem Behaviors at Home:

_____
_____
_____
_____

Specific Activity In the presence of adult or child	Before School	After School	Weekends	Other	Do you think the student's problem behavior is "to avoid something" or "to get something". Explain.
5 Extremely Intense					
4					
3					
2					
1 Not Intense					

Do you think your child's problem behavior is "to avoid something" or "to get something". Explain.

ABC's of RTI and Behavior
Functional Behavioral Assessment Interview *STUDENT* Form

This form can be used as a source to determine the function (reason) of a student's problem behavior. Interviews should be completed by multiple sources, e.g. parents/guardians, students (if appropriate), Intervention and/or IEP Team members, etc. in order to gather pertinent information to determine the function (reason) for a student's problem behavior. This information is to be used in conjunction with other data to develop and implement the behavior intervention plan based on findings from the functional behavioral assessment findings.

Respondent's Name: _____

Grade: _____   Age: _____   Date: _____

Check Title:
- ☐ Student/Self
- ☐ Student/Other: _____

1. Sometimes you get in trouble at school, is there something bothering you at home, school, or somewhere else? If so, tell me what it is?

2. Tell me what you feel about your behavior in school.

3. What do you think others (adults & peers) think about your behavior in school?

4. Is your problem behavior most likely occurring because you want to "get something" or "avoid something"?

5. What are you most likely trying to "get" or "avoid": 1) sensory/stimulation, 2) social (adult or peer attention), or 3) tangible/activity? Explain.

6. What would you like to see happen to fix the problem?

7. What do you like about school?

8. What don't you like about school?

9. What is your favorite subject in school? Why?

10. What is your least favorite subject in school? Why?

11. Who is your favorite person in school? Why?

12. Who is your least favorite person in school? Why?

13. Do you have high expectations for yourself? Do others? Explain.

14. What are you good at?

15. If you could make 3 wishes about anything, what would they be?

16. What kind of job or profession would you like to pursue when you finish school?

ABC's of RTI and Behavior
Functional Behavioral Assessment Interview *ADULT* Form

This form can be used as a source to determine the function (reason) of a student's problem behavior. Interviews should be completed by multiple sources, e.g. parents/guardians, students (if appropriate), Intervention and/or IEP Team members, etc. in order to gather pertinent information to determine the function (reason) for a student's problem behavior. This information is to be used in conjunction with other data to develop and implement the behavior intervention plan.

Student: _____ Date: _____

Grade: _____   Respondent's Name: _____

Check Title:

  ❑ Parent/Guardian

  ❑ Teacher/Content Taught: _____

  ❑ Paraprofessional

  ❑ Other: _____

1. Describe the problem behavior in observable and measurable terms (what does the behavior look like).

2. How often does the problem behavior occur, e.g. number of times per day, week, month, etc.?

3. How long does the problem behavior last, e.g. minutes per day, week, month, etc.?

4. On a scale of 1 to 10, how intense is the problem behavior 1 = Not intense; 10 = Extremely intense?

5. What activity/event is frequently taking place when the problem behavior occurs?

6. When is the problem behavior MOST likely to occur (time of day, day of week, etc.)?

7. When is the problem behavior LEAST likely to occur (time of day, day of week, etc.)?

8. Where is the problem behavior MOST likely to occur (time of day, day of week, etc.)?

9. Where is the problem behavior LEAST likely to occur (time of day, day of week, etc.)?

10. With whom is the problem behavior MOST likely to occur?

11. With whom is the problem behavior LEAST likely to occur?

12. Do you think the problem behavior occurs because the student wants to "get something" or "avoid something"?

13. Is the problem behavior most likely to get or avoid 1) sensory/stimulation, 2) social (adult or peer attention), or 3) tangible/activity? Explain.

14. What kind of event(s) most likely triggers the problem behavior?

15. What are the warning signs that the problem behavior is going to occur (antecedent)?

16. What typically happens after the problem behavior occurs (consequence)?

17. What most likely is the function (reason) for the student's problem behavior?

18. What appropriate behavior(s) could the student demonstrate within the same social/environmental context that would help the student, a) get the thing they are seeking or b) avoid the thing they are trying to escape?

19. What is the student's favorite subject?

20. What is the student's favorite activity outside of school?

21. What is motivating to the student?

22. Who are the student's friends?

23. What are the student's career interests?

24. Other comments:

Student Behavior Profile
Student Profile: *What are the student's greatest strengths and weaknesses?*
Target /Problem Behavior(s): *What is the student's specific problem behavior identified for increase or decrease?*   Description of Target/Problem Behavior(s) including duration, frequency and intensity: Target/Problem Behaviors Targeted for Increase: Target/Problem Behaviors Targeted for Decrease:
Outcome Goals: *Current Academic Performance: What is the student's current level of academic performance?*   *Academic Outcome Goal: What is the academic outcome goal? By when: 1 month, 3 months, etc.*   *Current Behavioral Performance: What is the student's current level of behavioral performance?*   *Behavioral Outcome Goal: What is the behavioral outcome goal? By when: 1 month, 3 months, etc.*

Analyzing Patterns of Behavior

Description of the problem behavior: Now describe the problem behavior using observable measurable terms (ex. Hits, kicks, bites, etc.)

Circumstances when the problem behavior is MOST likely to occur:
 	
    1. Where:
 	
    2. When:
 	
    3. With whom:

Circumstances when the problem behavior is LEAST likely to occur:
 	
    1. Where:
 	
    2. When:
 	
    3. With whom:

Why do think the problem behavior occurs:
 	
    1. To get something? If so, what?
 	
    2. To avoid something? If so, what?

Problem/Target Behaviors

Describe what the student's problem behavior looks like in observable measurable terms:

Approximately, how often does the problem behavior occur:

On a scale from 1 to 10 rate the severity of the problem behavior 1 = not severe; 10 = extremely severe. Then describe the intensity of the problem behavior.

Why do you think the behavior is occurring? Does the student lack specific academic and/or social/behavioral skills that may be causing the behavior? Or is the behavior occurring to get or avoid something? If so, what?

Scatter Plot

Student: _____

Observer: _____

Dates: _____ to _____

Target Behavior:

The use of a scatter plot involves recording the time of day, context/activity, and date in which the problem behavior does and does not occur in order to identify patterns of behavior. Selection of timeframe and intervals to observe the problem behavior should be carefully considered e.g. over 10 consecutive days, for 1 hour per day in 10 minute intervals. This information can be used in determining the function of behavior and further use with the development of a behavior intervention plan.

Time	Context/Activity	Dates									

☐ Behavior Did Not Occur

■ Behavior Occurred

N/A Did not observe

ABC Observation Form

Student: _____   Day & Date: _____
Observer: _____

Time (Beginning – Ending)	Context or Activities	Antecedent/ Setting Events	Identified Target Behavior	Consequence	Student Reaction
KEY	**KEY**	**KEY**	**KEY**	**KEY**
A: Reading	A: New Task	A: Out of Seat	A: Redirect	A: Continued
B: Lang. Arts	B: Transition	B: Hitting	B: Reprimand	B: Stopped
C: Math	C: Routine Task	C: Cursing	C: Peer Attention	C: Intensified
D: Science	D: Redirect	D: Throwing Objects	D: Adult Attention	D: Screamed
E: Soc. Stud.	E: Reprimand	E:	E: Removed from Activity	E: Left Room
F: P.E.	F: Told No	F:	F: Choice Given	F: Slept
G:	G: Choice Given	G:	G: Time Out	G:
H:	H: Ignore	H:	H:	H:
I:	I:	I:	I:	I:
J:	J:	J:	J:	J:
K:	K:	K:	K:	K:
L:	L:	L:	L:	L:
M:	M:	M:	M:	M:
N:	N:	N:	N:	N:

Functional Behavior Assessment
Identification Form

Target/ Problem Behavior	Predictors of Target/ Problem Behavior	Perceived Function of Behavior: • Get something: attention/adult; attention/peer; item/activity; sensory/self-stim • Escape something: demand/request; activity; person	Skill Problem or Performance Problem	Instruments Used to Determine Function of Behavior & Date: • Interviews • Checklists • Questionnaires • Data Analysis

Behavior Intervention/Support Plan

Student: _____   Date: _____

Identified Function of Behavior: _____

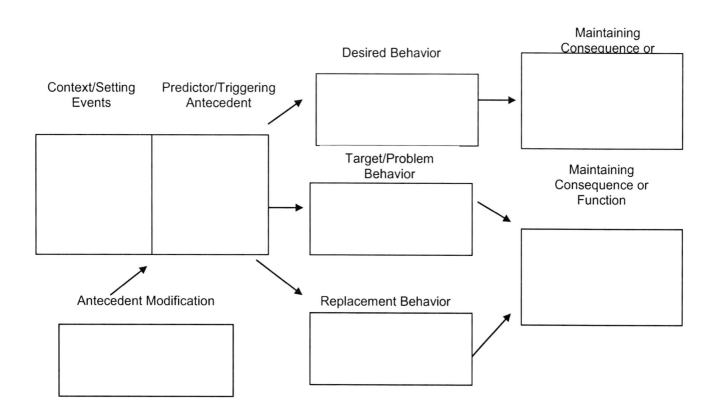

What are ways to change the context to make the problem behavior unnecessary?	What are ways to prevent the problem behavior?	What can be done to increase expected behaviors or to teach a replacement behavior?	What should happen when a problem behavior occurs?	What should happen when desired or replacement behavior occurs?

Annual Rate of Referral To
Special Education/Tier 3

School: _____   System: _____

Date: _____   School Year: _____

Name/Title of Person Completed Form: _____

Grade	Number Referred	Number Placed	Minority Referred	Minority Placed	Total in School	Total Percent Referred	% of Referred Students who are placed	% Minority Referred	% of Referred Minority Students Placed
1st									
2nd									
3rd									
4th									
5th									
Total									
Total Previous Year									

Annual Rate of Referral To
Special Education/Tier 3

School: _____   System: _____

Date: _____   School Year: _____

Name/Title of Person Completed Form: _____

Grade	Number Referred	Number Placed	Minority Referred	Minority Placed	Total in School	Total Percent Referred	% of Referred Students who are placed	% Minority Referred	% of Referred Minority Students Placed
6th									
7th									
8th									
Total									
Total Previous Year									

138

Annual Rate of Referral To
Special Education/Tier 3

School: _____   System: _____

Date: _____   School Year: _____

Name/Title of Person Completed Form: _____

Grade	Number Referred	Number Placed	Minority Referred	Minority Placed	Total in School	Total Percent Referred	% of Referred Students who are placed	% Minority Referred	% of Referred Minority Students Placed
9th									
10th									
11th									
12th									
Total									
Total Previous Year									

Chapter 7
PROGRESS MONITORING

Progress monitoring is the frequent assessment of students on specific academic or behavioral performance. Progress monitoring is conducted on a regular basis to determine whether students are benefiting from instruction. The frequency of progress monitoring typically depends on student's identified level of need, best practices, local school system resources, and federal and state recommendations.

Universal screening is different than progress monitoring. Universal screening is characterized by the quick administration and assessment of grade appropriate skills of all students. Universal screening measures are used to determine students' level of proficiency in essential content areas (ex. reading, math, behavior). Typically, schools administer screenings to all students three times per year once in the Fall, Winter, and Spring. Universal screening data are then analyzed for both group performance and individual student performance on specific skills. According to the National Association of State Directors of Special Education (2005) and the National Research Council on Learning Disabilities (2006), data gathered from universal screenings provide two types of information:

1. Functionality of the core curriculum and instruction within the school, provided that 80% or more of the students are making adequate progress in the core curriculum on a particular element or program. The remaining 20% of at-risk students will require additional intervention either in a small group or on an individual basis depending on the tier. But prior to providing more intensive interventions for the 20% of students not at benchmark, universal screenings may be repeated with these students to determine whether or not scores are due to skill deficits ("can't do" problems) or performance deficits ("won't do problems).
2. Identifies students who are not making acceptable progress in the core curriculum.

Progress monitoring is conducted more frequently than universal screenings and there are two primary types of progress monitoring (National Center on Progress Monitoring, 2007):

1. Curriculum based measurement (CBM)
2. Mastery measurement

Curriculum based measurement is the most popular type of progress monitoring. With CBM, teachers monitor what their students are expected to know by the end of the year and they assess their students on those skills frequently. Most of the work in CBM has been in the areas of reading, math, written expression, and spelling with elementary students.

With mastery measurement, teachers identify a set and sequence of objectives and monitor a student's progress by tracking student progress on each of the objectives. Of the two, mastery measurement is more appropriate to use to progress monitor behavior.

There are three basic reasons for progress monitoring a student's skill development:

1. Screening – this identifies how a student is performing relative to the group or to a curriculum based or behavioral benchmark
2. Diagnostic – to determine why a student is underperforming
3. On-going progress monitoring – frequent assessment of growth to determine effectiveness or resistance to intervention

It is extremely important to note that universal screening and progress monitoring are both extremely beneficial for their appropriate use. However, neither universal screening nor progress monitoring data tell us a student's academic or behavioral instructional level nor the specific skills needed to move forward. This requires digging deeper and analyzing the data to determine the specific need of each student so they can adequately progress in the curriculum and/or socially acceptable standards of behavior.

Purposes of Three Types of Assessment

	Screening	Progress Monitoring	Diagnostic Tests
Population	School-wide	Class/small group/student	Individual student
Uses	Broad Index Broad Index	Specific academic skill or behavioral target	Specific academic domains of knowledge, skills, or abilities
Frequency	Yearly/3x/monthly	≤ 3 weeks/weekly/daily	yearly
Purpose	Identify students who are at-risk	Regroup students	Identify specific students deficits
Focus	School focus	Student/class focus	Student focus
Instruction	Class/school instruction and curriculum decisions	Within intervention (curriculum/instruction)	Selecting curriculum and instructional methods
Implications	As first steps for intervention planning	Continue or revise placement	Planning or specifying intervention

(National Research Center on Learning Disabilities, www.nrcld.org, August 2006)

Steps Involved in the Progress Monitoring Process (National Center on Student Progress Monitoring, 2007):

1. Establish consistent benchmarks for grade level student performance and plot them on a chart (e.g., "read orally a grade level 45 words per minute by May" or complies with requests 4 out of 5 opportunities). It must be plotted at the projected end of the instructional period, such as the end of the school year.
2. Establish the student's current level of performance (e.g., "25 words per minute" or complies with requests 1 out of 5 opportunities).
3. Draw an aim line (goal line) from the student's current level of performance to the performance benchmark. This is a picture of the slope of progress required to meet the benchmark.
4. Monitor the student's progress using short term assessments at Tier 1. Monitor the student's progress using CBMs or mastery measurement at Tier 2, at least weekly. Plot the data.
5. Analyze the data on a regular basis applying decision rules established by research-based practices or state or district level criteria.
6. Draw a trend line to validate that the student's progress is adequate to meet the goal over time.

Data collected on all students should be discussed with the intervention team. The team is to examine the student's diagnostic data and determine if the student's needs are being met. The student's baseline is plotted along with the class benchmark and the team is to take into account other students' rate of progress. The line between where the student is and where the team wants the student to be is the student's aim line (goal line). If student performance falls significantly below the goal line over the course of three to four consecutive monitoring periods, the intervention team should revise the intervention plan to make appropriate changes so the student can make adequate progress towards established goals. These conversations regarding students' responsiveness to intervention and supporting data are inherent to the problem solving process.

Basic Problem Solving (Teachers and School Teams)
(Heartland Area Education Agency, Johnston, IA)

• **Define the Problem**
(Screening and Diagnostic Assessments)
What is the problem and why is it happening?

· **Evaluate**
(Progress Monitoring Assessment)
Did our plan work?

· **Develop a Plan**
(Goal Setting and Planning)

What are we going to do?

· **Implement Plan**
(Treatment Integrity)
Carry out the intervention

When using progress monitoring data and graphs to make determinations about the effectiveness of interventions, there are two basic decision rules to consider: 1) If there are three or four consecutive data points below the goal for the student's performance at the end of a pre-determined period of time (e.g., 4 to 6 weeks), a change in instructional strategies is needed; 2) If there are three or four consecutive data points above the aim line (goal line), the performance goal for the student is too low and needs to be raised. Once the student is consistently performing at grade level expectations or performance benchmark, the intervention team can consider phasing the interventions out. Robust progress monitoring procedures such as graphing results and using trend lines are needed in order to apply consistent decision rules. A great resource for establishing progress monitoring goals can be found at the website for the National Center on Student Progress Monitoring at: www.studentprogress.org.

Chapter 8
SPECIAL EDUCATION

With the advent of *No Child Left Behind (NCLB)* and *Response to Intervention (RTI)* many local school systems have implemented a multi-tiered service delivery model. Those using the three tier model of service delivery, the tertiary tier, has become synonymous with special education. Tier 3 represents more intensive levels of support rather than a final destination for students experiencing extreme academic and/or behavioral challenges. Tier 3 for students referred on and found eligible for special education includes, but is not limited to intensive, individualized, high-quality instruction matched to student need in addition to the supports provided at Tier 1 and Tier 2.

Special education services in the RTI model do not represent a location of services, but represent a layer of interventions that may be provided either in the general education classroom or in a separate setting. In the RTI model, special education services are intended to provide the most intensive scientifically based instructional programs that address individual student needs (Fuchs & Fuchs, 2006). There is more promise in the RTI model for students with disabilities than ever before, because RTI has more flexibility for students to move in and out of special education as their individual needs change in relation to their performance in the general curriculum. However, it is important to remember that RTI, as an instructional model, generates documentation that is required of all evaluations for special education services under every disability category. Additionally, it is important to remember that the dual discrepancy model is built specifically upon RTI generated student achievement data and provides only one component in the evaluation process. General special education evaluation requirements can be found in the IDEA at: http://idea.ed.gov/explore/home and specific evaluation requirements can be located from individual State Departments of Education.

Here are a few IDEA key provisions and changes in relation to initial evaluations and re-evaluations that have a direct link to the RTI process in determining eligibility for special education:

1. Review existing data provisions.

As part of an initial evaluation (if appropriate) and as part of any reevaluation under Part 300, the IEP Team and other qualified professionals, as appropriate, must:

- Review existing evaluation data on the child, including:
  o Evaluations and information provided by the parents of the child;
  o Current classroom based, local, or State assessments, and classroom-based observations; and
  o Observations by teachers and related services providers; and

- On the basis of that review, and input from the child's parents, identify what additional data, if any, are needed to determine:
  - o Whether the child is a child with a disability, as defined in 34 CFR 300.8, and the educational needs of the child; or, in case of a reevaluation of a child, whether the child continues to have such a disability, and the educational needs of the child;
  - o The present levels of academic achievement and related developmental needs of the child;
  - o Whether the child needs special education and related services; or, in the case of a reevaluation of a child, whether the child continues to need special education and related services; and
  - o Whether any additions or modifications to the special education and related services are needed to enable the child to meet the measurable annual goals set out in the IEP of the child and to participate, as appropriate, in the general education curriculum.

[34   CFR   300.305(a)]   [20   U.S.C.   1414(c)(1)-(4)]

The group described in 34 CFR 300.305(a) may conduct its review without a meeting.
[34   CFR   300.305(b)]   [20   U.S.C.   1414(c)(1)-(4)]

The public agency must administer such assessments and other evaluation measures as may be needed to produce the data identified under 34 CFR 300.305(a).
[34   CFR   300.305(c)]   [20   U.S.C.   1414(c)(1)-(4)]

If the IEP Team and other qualified professionals, as appropriate, determine that no additional data are needed to determine whether the child continues to be a child with a disability, and to determine the child's educational needs, the public agency must notify the child's parents of:

- That determination and the reasons for the determination; and
- The right of the parents to request an assessment to determine whether the child continues to be a child with a disability, and to determine the child's educational needs.

The public agency is not required to conduct the assessment described in 34 CFR 300.305(d)(1)(ii) unless requested to do so by the child's parents. [34 CFR 300.305(d)] [20 U.S.C. 1414(c)(1), (2), (4)]

2. Clarify that screening for instructional purposes is not evaluation.

The screening of a student by a teacher or specialist to determine appropriate instructional strategies for curriculum implementation shall not be considered to be an evaluation for eligibility for special education and related services. [34 CFR 300.302] [20 U.S.C. 1414(a)(1)(E)]

3.   Revise   provisions   regarding   determinant   factors.

A child must not be determined to be a child with a disability under Part B:

- If the determinant factor for that determination is:
  o Lack of appropriate instruction in reading, including the essential components of reading instruction (as defined in section 1208(3) of the ESEA);
  o Lack of appropriate instruction in math; or
  o Limited English proficiency; and
- If the child does not otherwise meet the eligibility criteria under 34 CFR 300.8(a).

[34   CFR   300.306(b)] [20   U.S.C.   1414(b)(5)] [34 CFR 300.301(c)] [20 U.S.C. 1414(a)(1)(C)]

As you know special education determination is to be taken seriously as eligibility impacts the lives of individuals for a lifetime. The IDEA 2004 governs eligibility decisions with requirements regarding multi-factored assessment and consideration of a variety of domains in placement decision making. 34 C.F.R. Section §300.304(b)(4). The IDEA states that, "the child is assessed in all areas related to the suspected disability". This process can be time consuming and costly, but ultimately beneficial to students when assessment and appropriate research-based interventions are put in place that are accurate, relevant, and implemented with fidelity.

The *"ABC's of RTI and Behavior"* was written as a step-by-step instructional manual to assist intervention teams apply and use the problem solving model to provide a well integrated system of instruction and interventions guided by student outcome data to make appropriate instructional decisions for students with behavioral and/or academic challenges. As you know, the purpose of the Individuals with Disabilities Education Act (IDEA, 2004) and the No Child Left Behind Act (NCLB, 2001) is to produce better educational outcomes for all children. It is my desire to make this process a bit easier, by providing a smidgen more guidance than most have received on doing the right thing for children and providing students with a true opportunity to succeed through teachers teaching and students responding as the open door for student success.

"The man who has done his level best…is a success, even though the world may write him down a failure".
B.C. Forbes

References

Access Center (2007). Retrieved December 12, 2007, from
http://www.k8accesscenter.org/index.php.

APlusMath (2007). Retrieved March 10, 2007, from http://www.aplusmath.com/.

Artiles, A. J., & Harry, B. (2004). *Addressing culturally and linguistically diverse student overrepresentation in special education: Guidelines for parents.* (Contract No. H326E020003). Denver, CO: National Center for Culturally Responsive Educational Systems.

Bender, W.N., & Shores, C. (2007). Response to intervention: A practical guide for every teacher. Thousand Oaks, CA: Corwin Press.

Best Evidence Encyclopedia (2007). Retrieved January 5, 2006, from
http://www.bestevidence.org/index.htm

Compton, D.L., Fuchs, D., & Fuchs, L.S. (2006, April). LD identification within an RTI model: An overvieew of the tiered service delivery model. Presentation at the National SEA Conference on SLD Determination: Integrating RTI within the SLD Determination Process, Kansas City, Mo. Retrieved July 12, 2006, from
http://www.nrcld.org/sea/presenations_worksheets/tsd/compton_tsd.pdf.

Compton, D.L., Fuch, D., Fuchs, L.S., & Bryant, J.D. (2006). Selecting at-risk readers in first grade for early intervention: A two-year longitudinal study of decision rules and procedures. Journal of Educational Psychology, 98, 394-409.

Connected Mathematics Project (2007). Retrieved July 14, 2007, from
http://www.connectedmath.msu.edu/.

Cool Math 4 Kids (2007). Retrieved September 23, 2007 from
http://www.coolmath4kids.com/.

DIBELS Data System (2006). Retrieved September 5, 2006, from
https://dibels.uoregon.edu/benchmark.php.

Donovan, S., & Cross. (2002). *Minority students in special and gifted education.* Washington, DC: National Academy Press.

Dr. Mac's Behavior Management Site (2007). Retrieved October 11, 2007, from
http://www.behavioradvisor.com/.

Edinformatics (2007). Retrieved April 1, 2007 from
    http://www.edinformatics.com/kids_teens/kt_math.htm

Education for All Handicapped Children's Act of 1975 (Public Law 94-142).

Elementary and Secondary Education Act of 1965 (Public Law 89-10).

Everyday Mathematics Center (2007). Retrieved April 21, 2007, from
    http://everydaymath.uchicago.edu/.

Figure This Math (2007). September 16, 2007 from
    http://www.figurethis.org/index.html.

Florida Center for Reading Research (2006). Retrieved March 14, 2006, from
    http://www.fcrr.org/.

Positive Behavior Support Project (2006). Retrieved January 13, 2006, from
    http://flpbs.fmhi.usf.edu/index.asp.

Florida's Positive Behavior Support Project (2006). Retrieved January 13, 2006,
    from http://flpbs.fmhi.usf.edu/index.asp.

Foundations for success: The final report of the national mathematics advisory
    panel (2008). Retrieved April 2, 2008, from
    http://www.ed.gov/about/bdscomm/list/mathpanel/index.html .

Fuchs, L.S., & Fuchs, D. (2006). Implementing responsiveness-to-intervention to
    identify learning disabilities. *Perspectives on Dyslexia, 32*(1), 39-43.

Garcia, S. B., & Ortiz, A. A. (1988). *Preventing inappropriate referrals of
    language minority students to special education* (New Focus Series, No.
    5). Wheaton, MD: National Clearninghouse for Bilingual Education.

Georgia Department of Education (2007). Implementation resource: Building
    capacity through best practices. Atlanta, GA: Georgia Department of
    Education

Georgia Department of Education (2007). Special education rules training:
    Eligibility determination *[34 C.F.R. § 300.306]*. Workshops presented
    across the state.

Garcia, S. B., & Ortiz, A. A. (1988). *Preventing inappropriate referrals of
    language minority students to special education* (New Focus Series, No.
    5). Wheaton, MD: National Clearninghouse for Bilingual Education.

Gresham, F. M., VanDerHeyden, A., & Witt, J. C. (2005). *Response to intervention of learning disabilities: Empirical support and future challenges* (frank.Gresham@ucr.edu). Riverside, CA: Frank M. Gresham, Graduate School of Education University of California-Riverside.

Gresham, F. M. (2004). Current status and future directions of school-based behavioral interventions. School Psychology Review, 33 (3), 326-343.

Hawkins, J.D., Catalano, R.F., Kosterman, R., Abbott, R., & Hill, K.G. (1999). Preventing adolescent health-risk behaviors by strengthening protection during childhood. *Archives of Pediatrics & Adolescent Medicine,* 13, 226-234.

Hilliard, A. G., III (2000). Excellence in education versus high-stakes standardized testing. *Journal of Teacher Education, 51,* 293-304.

ILIAD Project at NABSE. (2002). *Addressing over-representation of African-American students in special education.* Washington, DC: The National Alliance of Black School Educators.

Individuals with Disabilities Education Act of 1997 (Public Law 94-142).

Individuals with Disabilities Education Improvement Act of 2004 (Public Law 108-446).

Intervention Central (2007). Retrieved May 28, 2008, from http://www.interventioncentral.org/.

Jenkins, J.R. (2003, December). Candidate measures for screening at-risk students. Paper presented at the NRCLD Responsiveness-to-Intervention Symposium, Kansas City, MO. Retrieved April 3, 2006, from http://www.nrcld.org/symposium2003/jenkins/index.html.

Losen, D. J., & Orfield, G. (Eds.) (2002). *Racial inequity in special education.* Cambridge, MA: Harvard University Press.

Martens, B.K., & Meller, P.J. (1990). The application of behavioral principles to educational settings. In T.B.Gutkin & C.R.Reynolds (Eds)., *Handbook of School Psychology.* New York: John Wiley & Sons.

McCook, J.E. (2006). The RTI guide: Developing and implementing a model in your schools. Horsham, PA: LRP Publications.

National Association of State Directors of Special Education, Inc. (2005). *Response to intervention: Policy considerations and implementation.* Alexandria, VA: Author.

National Association of State Directors of Special Education, Inc. (2005). *Response to intervention: Policy considerations and implementation.* Alexandria, VA: Author.

National Reading Panel (2006). Retrieved April 15, 2006, from http://www.nationalreadingpanel.org/default.htm.

No Child Left Behind Act of 2001 (Public Law 107-110).

Managing Onsite Disciple for Effective Learning (2007). Retrieved June 14, 2007, from http://www.modelprogram.com/.

Marzano, R. J. (2003). What works in schools: Translating research into action. Alexandria, VA: Association for Supervision and Curriculum Development.

MathDrills (2007). February 2, 2007, from http://www.mathdrills.com/.

Math Forum at Drexel (2007). Retrieved August 9, 2007 from http://mathforum.orgarithmetic/arith.software.html.

Math Video Instructional Developmental Source (2007). Retrieved October 9, 2007, from http://coe.jmu.edu/mathvids2/.

National Association of State Directors of Special Education (NASDSE), Inc. (2005). *Response to Intervention: Policy Considerations and Implementation.* Alexandria, VA.

National Center for Culturally Responsive Educational Systems (2005). Retrieved January 13, 2005 from http://www.nccrest.org/.

National Center on Student Progress Monitoring (2007). Retrieved July, 7, 2007, from http://www.studentprogress.org/.

National Library of Virtual Manipulatives (2006). Retrieved June 13, 2006, from http://nlvm.usu.edu/.

National mathematics advisory panel (2008). *Foundations for success: The national mathematics advisory panel final report.* Washington, DC: U.S. Department of Education.

National Research Center on Learning Disabilities (2006). Retrieved August 9, 2006, from www.nrcld.org.

National Research Council on Learning Disabilities (NRCLD). (2006). *Integrating RtI Within the SLD Determination Process.* National SEA Conference on SLD Determination, Kansas City: April, 2006.

Nelson, J.R., Bennen, G.J., Reid, R.C., & Espstein, M.H. (2002). Convergent validity of officediscipline referrals with the CBCL-TRF. *Journal of Emotional & Behavioral Disorders 10*(3) 181-88.

Office of Special Education Programs National Technical Assistance Center on Positive Behavioral Intervention & Supports (2007). Retrieved November 20, 2007, from http://www.pbis.org/main.htm

Otter Creek Institute (2007). Retrieved November 20, 2007, from http://www.oci-sems.com/.

Peer Assisted Learning Strategies (2006). Retrieved January 2, 2006, from http://kc.vanderbilt.edu/pals/.

Positive Behavioral Interventions and Supports (2006). Retrieved February 15, 2007, from http://www.pbis.org/main.htm.

Project FORUM at NASDSE. (1997). *Addressing disproportionate representation of students from racial and ethnic minority groups in special education: A comprehensive examination.* Alexandria, VA: The National Association of State Directors of Special Education.

Read Write Think (2007). Retrieved August 9, 2007, from http://www.readwritethink.org/.

RTI Tools: A Response to Intervention Directory (2007). Retrieved December 22, 2007, from http://www.rtitools.com/.

Sprague, J., Cook, C.R., Wright, D.B., & Sadler, C. (2007). RTI and behavior: A guide to integrating behavioral and academic supports. Horsham, PA: LRP Publications.

Star Fall (2007). Retrieved August 1, 2007, from http://www.starfall.com/.

Sprague, J., Cook, C.R., Wright, D.B., & Sadler, C. (2007). RTI and behavior: A guide to integrating behavioral and academic supports. Horsham, PA: LRP Publications.

Sugai, G., Horner, R.H., & Gresham, F. (2002). Behaviorally effective environments. In Walker, Shinn, & G. Stoner (Eds.), Interventions for academic and behavior problems II: Preventative and remedial approaches. Bethesda, MD: National Association for School Psychologists.

Technical Assistance Center on Social Emotional Intervention for Young Children (2007). Retrieved February 12, 2007, from http://www.challengingbehavior.org/.

TutorNext (2007). Retrieved May 4, 2007, from http://www.tutornext.com/.

University of South Florida Problem Solving and Response to Intervention Project. (2007). Retrieved May 31, 2007 from http://floridarti.usf.edu/resources/index.html.

U.S. Department of Education (2005). Retrieved January 5, 2005 from http://www.ed.gov/about/landing.jhtml.

Video Math Tutor (2007). Retrieved October 10, 2007, from http://www.videomathtutor.com/.

What Works Clearinghouse (2007). Retrieved August 5, 2007, from http://ies.ed.gov/ncee/wwc/.

Wright, J. (2007). RTI toolkit: A practical guide for schools. Port Chester, NY: Dude Publishing.

Vaugh, S. Roberts, G. (2007). Secondary interventions in reading: Providing additional instruction for students at risk. Teaching Exceptional Students, 39(5), 40-46.

Printed in the United States
148555LV00001B/3/P